Praise for
Reclaim Your Space with
G.R.A.C.E.

What a fun, light read! I loved reading this book—it met me on multiple occasions. I love the incorporation of scripture, very inspiring and also practical. Some of these I had never even heard. I love that the book and system doesn't feel overwhelming or heavy.

Brittany Wirthlin
Author of *Molly Makes a Friend* & Marketing Professional

Let me just say that I love it. I think it will be so helpful to anyone who reads it. I love your practical process, but I also love how you have tied it back to the Lord and making Him and His purposes our focus. You help to clear the physical clutter but also the mental/emotional clutter tied to material things that keep us stuck.

Kristi Campbell
Mom Extraordinaire

Reclaim Your Space with G.R.A.C.E. is not only a self-help book, but a beautiful narrative and devotional outlining how to organize by setting attainable goals and giving the reader the grace and tools to tailor the plan to his or her specific needs with ease. Melinda shares personal moments along the way, which are relatable and encouraging. Organizing is hard work, and by sharing her experiences and pro tips, her strategy to reclaim your space comes to life! Don't wait any longer; now is the time and this is the strategy to tackle your space!

Kathy Caldwell
Mother of my Niece & Nephew

Melinda Grace offers an empowering and uplifting approach to organizing! A fantastic guide for anyone looking to reinvigorate their surroundings!

Lalita Kalayana
Massage Therapist, Mobile Massage Therapy

I absolutely loved this book and highly recommend it! Melinda's graceful approach makes each organizing step feel thoughtful and caring. I especially enjoyed the personal stories she shared, including her own experiences. I'll definitely be using this book to reclaim my spaces!

Debbie Morgan, CPA
Deborah Morgan & Company, Inc.

This book is gold! I consider myself a pretty organized person and found lots of gems inside. Melinda's guidance makes the process so easy, which takes away some of the overwhelm that often comes with decluttering and organizing. My two favorite parts of the book were the reminder of prepping before starting and the section on release. I teach my clients how to release emotions and thoughts that no longer serve them. Releasing 'things' that no longer serve is also SO important. This book is a must-read for those new to organizing as well as those who are self-proclaimed as being organized. There is something for all levels.

Glennda Donate, CMLC
Master Certified Life Coach

This book is amazing!!! Melinda structures her book as a 6-week course—a 6-week Boot Camp Challenge for the soul. Not only does it give helpful hints on decluttering and organizing, but it touched my soul and dug deep into the emotional and psychological reasons why we hold onto things and why we are afraid to let go. Much of Melinda's thought process rang true for me. She writes in a way that is completely free of judgement—rather, her focus is on helping, healing, and inspiring. For those of us who struggle with clutter and are overwhelmed by disorganized spaces, this book is a Godsend, literally!!! Melinda writes from the heart, with love and empathy. Her examples show her passion to help others, no matter the size of the space or the budget. It's as if she takes the reader by the hand, acknowledging any dilemma that may spring up, and gently guides you through the process. She combines her own personal experiences with "coaching sessions" and spiritual verses or quotes from other writers. The spirituality of her book gives strength and encouragement to the reader, supporting any task, big or small, with personal prayers and calls to self-reflection. I highly recommend this book to anyone who feels "stuck" or overwhelmed by clutter, a disorganized home or office, or just needs someone in their corner. Thank you, Melinda, for a beautifully written book!!!

Nicole Coates
Graphic Designer, Nicole Coates, Inc.

For me, just the idea of decluttering often feels like too much, which is why I read this book. This book is a gentle reprieve and a solution. From the G.R.A.C.E. acronym for step-by-step assistance to overall theme of love and grace, this book is the gentle nudge I needed to organize a closet I had been avoiding. Thank you!

Bonnie Lippincott
Podcaster, Entry Level Mom

Reclaim Your Space with G.R.A.C.E. reads a lot like Melinda's personality—warm, approachable and full of insights and fun stories. Managing a household and everything in it takes courage, vision and faith, and this book is so helpful to not only support those inner attitudes and mindsets but also to offer transformative truth from the Creator and Sustainer of the entire universe! Wow, what an opportunity; to not simply exist around our stuff but to claim it and form it in the way that God has formed the world and is forming us.

Cortney Matz
Artist & Creative Coach, Cortneymatz.com

When I took Melinda Grace's online organizing course and hired her to help me organize my classroom, she came alongside me as a dear friend, encouraging and instilling "a sense of ease and confidence in (my) organizing journey" as she so aptly describes in her book. As you read, *Reclaim Your Space with G.R.A.C.E.*, you too will find a true friend guiding you through the organizing process with G.R.A.C.E. and to the only One who can save us from the chaos and empower us "to have life and have it to the full." (John 10:10 NIV)

Laurie Arriaga
Educator

RECLAIM YOUR SPACE
WITH
G.R.A.C.E.

A FAITH-BASED
ORGANIZING JOURNEY

Melinda Grace

DEDICATION

I'd like to dedicate this book to God and my parents because when everyone else gave up on me, they were there waiting with open arms. I would not be where I am today without their grace, love and compassion. To my parents, whose prayers saved me and whose home nurtured me.

GRATITUDE

I would like to acknowledge and thank several people who have helped, influenced and inspired me to make this book a reality:

My husband—the love of my life

Family & Friends:
Kathy Caldwell, Andre Diniz, Gayle Wirthlin, Brittany Wirthlin, Kristi Campbell

Editor & Friend:
Amanda McMullen—who helped my voice and heart sing with perfect grammar.

Mentors:
Kathy Young Deegan—who helped me find my place in this world and Ruth Klein—who helped my book find its place in this world.

My amazing clients who inspired me to write a fun and inspirational book on organizing.

CONTENTS

INTRODUCTION

What do you do when the anxieties of life catch up to you and you can't see a way out? Where do you go when a life transition knocks you down and you're surrounded by clutter—mentally, emotionally, and physically?

It's January of 2019 in Los Angeles. I'm submitting for acting roles in my shabby chic studio apartment at my super cute, chalk-painted, meticulously organized desk. Then—*ding*. An email alert from my bank informs me that my checking account hit below $100. *Oh, no!* In addition, my contract is up with my employer, which means I'm out of a job. With no savings, and no other job, acting or business lined up, my heart drops into my stomach.

I am a Texas gal living in Southern California (SoCal), where I moved to "make it" on the big screen in Hollywood. Prior to moving to SoCal, I lived the most amazing, single life in New York City! I had incredible friends, a flexible job, and was being cast all the time in plays. I became the go-to for ingénue roles in classic theatre. And *I loved it*. I spent my downtime exploring the city, seeing shows, and learning about life. I found my voice as a person and artist in New York City, which is the journey I shared in my sold-out solo show in 2018 at the Hollywood Fringe Festival.

In 2014, I left New York City for a myriad of reasons, but mainly because it never felt like "home." I moved to Los Angeles to continue to pursue my dream of an acting career and also find a place that felt like "home." Back to the $100-in-my-bank notice. I console myself: *I have* *an agent who loves me. I attend a hip, "cool" church. I have a new supportive boyfriend, Jon, and am in love for the FIRST time. I'm getting called back in for Netflix shows and movies with celebrities. $100 in my bank account? I'm fine. It's all going fine. Just keep chasing your dreams, Melinda. List out your goals. Cross them off. Go to this networking event. Go to that party. Volunteer on this friend's film project. Memorize lines for acting class. Don't be late for improv. Drive to Culver City for an audition. Dress the part. Fix your hair. Smile. Hold the last beat for 3 secs. "N-B-C." Say thank you and leave. Be chatty. But not too chatty. Be yourself. No, be the character.*

This is my life on loop for three years: constantly feeling nervous and worried, calling home almost every week, crying. Despite my list of things "going for me," I'm not doing a good job of developing deep, meaningful friendships, and I'm not getting cast in anything that PAYS. I feel like a ticking-time bomb inside, yet I keep telling myself, "everything is going to be fine." Now, my legs shake when I go into auditions. I feel like I'm going to throw up. I try every trick in the book to trick my brain to focus on what I can do. I start to hear and believe that I am powerful. I believe that I can do it ALL, all by myself—and my solo show is going to prove it.

At last, a sold-out performance. A moment of relief. I am once again finding my identity and voice. Just one small catch: I don't love acting anymore. I no longer find solace in it. The solo show was artistically fulfilling, but I don't laugh or connect with other theatre folk, and financially the ROI is terrible. . . . And now, no steady job nor one coming my way. This leads me into a tailspin to find a career—and myself—FAST!

I go on a ton of job interviews, change my resume a million times to get that SEO just right, and decide to launch my career in digital marketing. I land several jobs, hate them, and immediately quit. Anxious, I take the next position I'm offered on my path to self-discovery in social media marketing for a film distribution company with big name celebrities. This dream job turns into a literal nightmare for me. Without really doing any research prior to accepting the position, I realized that they produce horror films. I loathe horror films. Just looking at the images creeps me out and gives me nightmares. But to do my job well, I need to watch these movies! My heart starts to beat hard in my chest, tears welling up inside. I feel like I have made the wrong job choice. Again.

Determined for this not to be true, I load up on coffee, go into the office early, leave late and stay up until midnight most nights working—all the time panicking that they would find out I was a fraud and regret they'd hired me. This fear drives me insane day and night for almost a month until one Sunday night I feel lightheaded. I can't stop crying. My body is shaking. All I ever wanted to do is act, but this role was too much. I hate it here. Should I move home to Houston? Should I quit *another* job?

I'm alone in my apartment and don't know what else to do, except to go home. I am not thinking clearly. I panic and am terrified. I call my parents, pack my bags, say goodbye to my three-year boyfriend, Jon, and drive home to Houston, TX. I don't listen to the radio, I don't look at social media, I don't talk to anyone. I just stare into the countryside and drive. West Texas never looked so pretty and inviting. No people. No noise. Just God's creation and open land for as far as my eyes can see.

I make it home, my parents accept me with open arms, and I go to my room and cry. As I begin to process what had happened, I learned that I was experiencing an anxiety attack. I discovered that it is extremely prevalent in America. I'm shocked. Why is this so common and yet no one in my life or social sphere had ever talked about anxiety before? Was social media to blame? Was I to blame? Maybe it was all of it.

I stay home in Houston for about two months, resting and spending time with God, family and friends. I quit that job; and Jon—for reasons I'll never understand—stayed in touch and encouraged me. I finally admitted to myself that I can't do life in my own power and by my own ideals. I confessed that I was *not* in control, and that I can't pull myself up by the bootstraps and make IT happen. Whatever IT is. I realized I'd been hiding from my faith and running from job to job, forging my own path ahead out of fear instead of really seeking Him and coming from a place of peace and rest. I acknowledged that acting had changed from a gift to an idol. Despite all of this, God forgave me, my self-reliance, and my desire to "make it" and serve Hollywood instead of Him. He had mercy on me and showered me with love.

Feeling revived and missing the love of my life, I go back to Los Angeles and officially stop acting, panicking, and rushing. I start to trust the process. I get married, find work, and take time to look back on my *entire* life, not just the one where I was an actress. I work with a vocational career coach and get down and dirty, digging into my past to see what layers were there waiting to be unearthed.

Fun fact: I *love* archeological TV shows and how today's technology allows us to discover new history from ages ago. And so, whilst recovering from the most anxiety-ridden season of my life, I excavate my soul, my history, my emotions, and my memories. It is painful and equally thrilling. I dig and dig and dig.

In the digging, I remember how, even as a child, I would organize my toys and dolls, and how important decorating my room was to me. I remember how much I loved nice things, and how I had these beautiful ceramics of different animals that I adored. I remember how completely crushed I was when, one day while vacuuming, they all fell and broke. I remember how I loved to design and organize all my dollhouses. I even had a "Dollhouse Town" in the game room of our house. I remember how much I loved being outside, daydreaming, and working with my hands. And then in a lightning moment, as if from God, I remember my dad telling me, "I don't know how you see where to put things away." In that instant, I know becoming a professional organizer is my next path.

Still, I dig. I remember how much I loved to travel. How from early on in my childhood, I traveled often, from church camps to family vacations to road trips, mission trips, and ski trips. I remember how I couldn't ever live in one place for very long before itching to meet new people and experience different cultures. I remember how I've lived in everything from a three-story house to a closet to a communal bunkbed situation. And with each new place, I spent hours and hours organizing and decorating—and then reorganizing and redecorating—even if it was just a bed and a wall.

All these different types of experiences involved different types of organizing and a unique ability to adapt and be creative. Then, it dawns on me, maybe that verse in the Bible that says "He works all things out for the good to those who love Him" might be true. Can He really take ALL of my newly excavated discoveries and use them in a career to help people?

I realize that I had navigated most of my life with a mixture of creativity, organization, compassion, faith, and adventure, and that I am at a crossroads: one where, if I take the leap, God could literally use everything in my life as a career and as a blessing to others.

I'm reminded of how I spent the last 10-15 years slowly going through all of my childhood memorabilia and going through the process any normal professional organizer would do with a client, except I wasn't one. Yet, I knew instinctively what to do. How to go through each item and decide what to do with it. Could this mean that I could relate to future clients downsizing? I hear myself shout,"*YES!*"

The discovery of the century is that, in all of my acting pursuits, I was also very organized, methodical, and creative. My entertainment experiences taught me to how to organize, write, and produce my own solo show and an award-winning short film. I knew I could use all of that in starting and marketing an organizing business. And that's exactly what I do! I open my professional organizing business in 2020 right smack dab in the middle of a global pandemic and have had a steady stream of clients ever since.

At the heart of this excavation story is a Heavenly Father (and family and friends) who did not give up on me. Even after years of selfish ambition, He graciously called me home to do some digging. Just like in organizing, I had to pull everything out and declutter my past, my memories, my experiences, my hurts, my joys—all of it. I've kept the most precious items and released what is no longer serving my new journey. In a nutshell, with the help of God and others, I decluttered and organized my life. In one of the toughest seasons, Grace called me home to a place of restoration and renewal.

Looking back, I see how I never lost track of my faith and how grace and home never lost track of me. When I started my organizing business in 2020, I knew grace, home and faith had to be incorporated into everything I do. The lessons I learned from this experience will undoubtedly express themselves in this book.

This process can help you create a gracious home of spaciousness that helps to bring peace, inspiration, and a newfound connection to your Creator. My goal is to teach you how to reclaim your space with G.R.A.C.E. Each chapter will take a deep-dive into the acrostic:

Gather

Release

Acquire

Cultivate

Enjoy

By the end of this book, my prayer is that if you put into practice the process laid out for you, your space will be a delight, and you will revel in God's grace more than you ever have before. By implementing the organizing process, you will experience more time, more energy, more room for new experiences, freedom, peace, and calm. On a logistical level, you will be able to find things and put things away when and where you need to, and you'll be able to do it with grace and ease.

Ready to reclaim your space with G.R.A.C.E.?

WEEK ONE

SOUL AND MIND DECLUTTERING

*"Therefore, since we are surrounded by such a huge cloud of witnesses to the life of faith, let us strip off **every weight** (emphasis mine) that slows us down, especially the sin that so easily trips us up."*

Hebrews 12:1 (NLT)

Since I was a child, I've always organized anything and everything around me. I'm still on this journey. Even today, as I write this, I'm in my parent's house thinning out toys and memories from my childhood. I've shed a lot of physical items over the years and come to see that sometimes these items symbolize our deepest fears and insecurities about ourselves and others.

The Bible says, "Therefore, since we are surrounded by such a huge cloud of witnesses to the life of faith, let us strip off **every weight** (emphasis mine) that slows us down, especially the sin that so easily trips us up" (Hebrews 12:1 NLT). I've learned first-hand that physical items can literally be a weight that hinders the lives we envision for ourselves and the calling God has for us.

Because of this weight, the process of decluttering can be difficult. I get it! It can bring up pain from the past and reveal our weaknesses. But in my experience, it helps to melt away anxiety and bring peace and clarity of vision. Simply put, the process can bring healing.

This week we are going to prepare the way for change, forward movement, and reclaiming our space with G.R.A.C.E. First, let me say that "owning things" in and of itself is not bad. In fact, God blessed many in the Old Testament by multiplying their physical land and possessions (Gen 24:34-35). It's when this abundance turns into a mental or physical burden that it becomes a problem for us. When the abundance clouds our connection with the Creator, it becomes detrimental for our souls.

Let's get started on literally stripping off physical, mental, and soul clutter! Let's learn how to **Reclaim *Your Space* with G.R.A.C.E.!**

FACT

". . . getting organized can also improve anxiety-related symptoms, 'as being disorganized is associated with higher levels of anxiety.'" [1]

Neha Khorana, Psychologist

TRUTH HURTS

For a few minutes, let's simply become aware of the vastness of our nationwide clutter phenomenon. Did you know that one in four Americans has a clutter problem and that the average American home contains 300,000 items[2]? We are drowning in a proverbial sea of "things" in our homes. The BBC reported that "[s]o many of us have so much stuff today, in fact, that a team of anthropologists at the University of California, Los Angeles (UCLA) have decided [. . .] that we are living in the most materially rich society in global history, with light-years more possessions per average family than any preceding society."[3] Ryan Rush, Pastor of Kingsland Baptist Church in Katy, Texas, said, "We are a nation that knows how to consume massive amounts of everything from TV to stuff to food."[4] He continues, "Too much consumption in any area can lead to misery in other areas of life."

What's even more concerning is that, according to a recent report, a huge number of these items end up in landfills, which "results in the waste of precious resources and pollution that threatens our health, environment and the global climate."[5]

Another startling statistic to consider, as I live near and love the ocean and all of its majestic creatures, is that "an estimated 16.5 million tons of plastic washes into the world's oceans every year. This plastic persists for hundreds of years and can kill marine animals … Marine debris is considered one of the great threats to biodiversity."[6] As believers, we are called to care for and respect God's creation. Consider the benefits of being in nature for the human psyche. Just hearing the ocean is linked to reduced stress and increased calmness.[7] None of us intend to harm this vital resource to our soul's health and happiness. I know that this subject isn't always comfortable because it's often politically polarizing, but I'd love for us to consider also looking at the organizing process as way to be good stewards of the abundance we have been blessed with while keeping the earth and its finite resources in mind.

WHY CLUTTER?

One interesting thing I've noticed from working with my clients is that they are often baffled by how the accumulation of items even happened in the first place. While some of it may be intentional, often there is an internal subconscious reason. Many times, clutter accumulates when there's been a life transition (e.g., moving), a traumatic experience (e.g., a medical situation), or perhaps trauma that has led to a mental illness, such as depression. A client of mine had lost both parents several years prior to our working together. It took five years, but she was finally ready to go through the items left to her and make tough decisions. The items had gathered in a closet from floor to ceiling. And that's how it happens! A major life event happens, you need time to process it, and the clutter builds up.

There's also an external subconscious reason, which as a former marketer, I find fascinating. That's what is termed "neuromarketing." Neuromarketing takes advantage of the subconscious decision-making process of consumers.[8] It leverages both neuroscience and psychology to predict consumer behavior, preferences, and motivations, which informs the entire go-to-market campaign. That's right! Some (or perhaps many) of the items we've accumulated in our homes have come in based on subconscious decisions that were designed by ingenious marketers. So, to that I say, give yourself some GRACE!

One example of how items magically appear in our homes is the freebies businesses give away so that you remember their company and spend money buying their products or services. Personally, I'm a sucker when I go the mall—so many subconscious messages happening. Plus, the endorphins that kick in when I actually buy something! It's hard to resist. It's always good to pause and consider, "Am I buying this item because I need it, or am I being emotionally driven?"

WHAT IS CLUTTER?

According to Joseph Ferrari, a professor of psychology at DePaul University in Chicago, "Clutter is an overabundance of possessions that collectively create chaotic and disorderly living spaces [. . .] Clutter can induce a physiological response, including increased levels of cortisol, a stress hormone."[9] One physician challenges us to consider that "mental and emotional clutter can hold just as much unnecessary space as physical clutter."[10]

There is also ". . . a growing body of evidence that clutter can negatively impact mental well-being, particularly among women [. . .] women who have issues with clutter have the signature pattern of cortisol that is associated with people who have chronic fatigue, post-traumatic stress disorder, and a higher risk of mortality."[11] No wonder most of my clients are female!

Clutter can also waste your time and money. Americans spend two and a half days a year looking for lost items and spend $2.7 billion a year replacing misplaced possesions.[12] It can also impact your social life by creating a resistance and embarrassment to having friends and family over to your home. Less community and human interaction can lead to loneliness, depression, and anxiety. "Social isolation's adverse health consequences range from sleeplessness to reduced immune function. Loneliness is associated with higher anxiety, depression, and suicide rates. Isolation and loneliness are also linked to poor cardiovascular health and cognitive function."[13]

I've had a couple of clients that hired me to help them get their house in order so that they would feel comfortable inviting friends over. We made so much progress that one client was able to have a friend stay with her and her husband for Thanksgiving. I was so proud of her!

MINDFULNESS

I want to share a story of how truly life-changing organizing can be when we also pay attention to our thoughts. In 2016, something in me was ready to find my person, and I started to take dating seriously. I was writing my solo show and doing intense work on my inner self when I realized that I didn't really like my wardrobe nor the shape my body was in. Certain clothes when I looked at them made me feel ugly . . . or fat . . . or sad, or—you know the thoughts I'm talking about that hit you like a wave when you stare at the clothes in your closet!

I also noticed that I had so many negative thoughts around finding love and dating. At the time, I was reading and listening to Dr. Pat Allen (whom I highly recommend if you're looking for love), and one of her main teaching points stood out to me:

"Beware of your thoughts for they become your words. Beware of your words for they become your actions. Beware of your actions for they become your character. Beware of your character, for it becomes your destiny." - Dr. Pat Allen

Determined to change my thoughts starting from the outside in: I decluttered my closet, started working out and eating healthy, and invested in clothes that made me feel like a million bucks. I got so into it that I decluttered, organized, and styled my entire studio apartment in a way that was totally me and would also attract the man that I desperately desired. And . . . it worked! I met the man of my dreams a few months later.

Our surroundings can send us millions of tiny subconscious messages—good and bad. You can change your thoughts! This is why it is also important to declutter our minds. To notice if there's anything from the get-go creeping in and cramping our style. Maybe these thoughts can be worked on from the inside out or maybe, like me, starting with a drawer or room and working from the outside in will be a miracle worker.

THE POWER OF ORGANIZING

In October of 2020, Jackie found me online in desperate need of decluttering and organization. The whole world is in the middle of a pandemic and like most of the world, Jackie was stuck at home. She has two kids of her own. She is also being a good Samaritan and taking care of a relative's three other children in a three-bedroom apartment. She decided to homeschool, write a book, get back into shape, and organize her home. All at the same time! So we needed to create order out of chaos with zones for her to teach, write, and ride her exercise bike.

Mission accepted. I show up to my first session, and it's literally mass chaos everywhere. She doesn't smile. She tends to me in order to get me going and then returns to cooking lunch, feeding the cat, and finishing laundry. I start in the area that is stressing her out the most and begin with the process you're going to learn about in this book. We had several sessions together and while I pulled everything out, sorted, purged, and organized, I overhear her teaching her children, writing and getting coached on her book, plus creating time to go through the items she uncovered with me.

A lot of items weren't very easy to review or make decisions about, as her father had just passed away. She did great working with me, speaking with me, figuring out which items needed to stay and which were not serving her anymore. I noticed that before each time I came back for another session, she had done additional work of going through other areas of her home that we didn't have time or budget for—sorting them, purging, and deciding to release many items that would end up in my trunk to go to the charity of her choice.

By the time we complete our organizing projects together, she had finished and published her book, those three extra spunky kiddos were able to return to their home, her kids had a routine, she was exercising, and she smiled . . . a lot. I could tell she was finding a new purpose in this "new normal." Shedding things from her past were critical in her journey of moving forward.

Did all those great things happen solely because she organized her home? Maybe, maybe not. She was determined for change and had a supportive family cheering her on. Did de-cluttering and organizing shift an energy in her, in her space and with her kids? Absolutely. Did God show up and meet her where she was as she created more physical space to hear Him speak? Absolutely. She knew something was wrong inside and out, and this client sought out healthy, spiritual and physical ways to heal and move forward.

Yes. Organizing can be that powerful.

PRAYER

I believe that distraction and isolation caused by a cluttered home can create a cavern in our souls, keeping us from hearing God's voice and being present with ourselves and those we love. I recommend the Christian author, Emily P. Freeman. She wrote a book and has a podcast called "The Next Right Thing." She speaks of "Soul Minimalism," a way to take care of your soul. She asks us, "How am I regularly getting rid of soul clutter I no longer need?" "What would a decluttered soul look like?" And she encourages us that, "Stillness is to the soul as de-cluttering is to the home."[14]

Before we embark on this incredible journey of reclaiming our physical spaces, I want us to take some time to be still and declutter our souls so that we can experience all God has for us over the next six weeks.

The Bible verse God laid on my heart for this book is, "Therefore, since we are surrounded by such a huge cloud of witnesses to the life of faith, let us strip off **every weight** (emphasis mine) that slows us down, especially the sin that so easily trips us up. And let us run with endurance the race God has set before us" (Hebrews 12:1-2 NLT). That's my prayer: that this book would give you the basic tools to help you get started on literally stripping off the physical and mental clutter by organizing your physical spaces to help you restore your inspiration, renew your mindset, and *Reclaim Your Space with G.R.A.C.E.!*

Let's take a minute to pray through three things:

1. Lord, we ask that you come and restore inspiration in our homes. "Restore to me the joy of your salvation and grant me a willing spirit, to sustain me" (Psalm 51:12 NIV). Restore our mental health as we organize the abundance we have; relieve the stress and anxiety that chaos can cause. "Be anxious for nothing, but in everything by prayer and supplication, with thanksgiving, let your requests be made known to God; and the peace of God which surpasses all understanding, will guard your hearts and minds through Christ Jesus" (Philippians 4:6-8 NKJV).

2. We ask for your help to stop conforming to the patterns of this world that can include over-abundance, unthoughtful discarding, and unintentional pollution and waste. "Don't copy the behavior and customs of this world, but let God transform you into a new person by changing the way you think" (Romans 12:2 NLT). Father, we ask for forgiveness for the ways we've unknowingly harmed the environmental home you gave us. Help us become more aware of our contribution to the problem and ways we can make changes.

3. Father, lastly, we ask for your help in reclaiming our space(s) so that they will be places of order, peace, rest, hope, community, love, and laughter. Give us strength when it gets tough to press on! ". . . Forgetting the past and looking forward to what lies ahead, I press on to reach the end of the race and receive the heavenly prize for which God, through Christ Jesus, is calling us" (Philippians 3:13-14 NLT). In Jesus' name, amen.

ENVISION

Are you ready? Do you feel the presence of God holding space for you to conquer your clutter? Then, let's pick a space or spaces to reclaim with G.R.A.C.E.! Close your eyes, take three deep breaths, then take a walk through your house in your mind. What space or spaces are stressing you out the most? What space(s) are hindering you? Why?

Now envision that space completely organized, styled, and clean. What does it look like? How does it smell? How does it make you feel to be in it? Feel it in your body. Take one last breath in, exhale, and open your eyes.

REFLECT

Journal. Let's reflect on that exercise. Take out your personal journal, or the companion journal to this book, which is available at www.melindagrace.com/grace, or simply any piece of paper. Take some time to write about all the feelings and emotions that come up for you as you envisioned your reclaimed space(s). Then answer the following questions:

1. What space are you reclaiming?

2. Is the clutter in this room causing you stress and anxiety?

3. Choose one word to describe how your (imagined) newly organized space made you feel.

4. What great things are you wanting to accomplish in your space now that it's organized?

How do you feel? Refreshed? Relieved that you don't have to go through this process alone? You may have noticed that just by the thought of simply getting your home organized, you feel lighter, happier, or calmer. I believe that's because God is the originator of order. He is the creator of order and systems, and we are made in His image. "So God created human beings in his own image. In the image of God he created them" (Gen. 1:27 NLT). That is why starting with our souls and minds and allowing Him to show us the possibilities and ways to organize our chaos is crucial to transforming your home and elevating your life.

It is my hope and prayer that dealing with our physical spaces and the objects that impact us every day will be a healthy and positive way to approach the unhealthy tactics we've been using to handle the stresses of life. It is just one piece to the puzzle. If at any point in the process you feel you need to stop and seek emotional and mental support, don't feel silly or stupid. Decluttering can be a very emotional process, and it is 100% OK to reach out to a friend, coach or therapist. I've listed some resources on my website to help if you get stuck.

DEEP DIVE

At the end of each chapter, I will give you action steps to take that will keep your journey moving forward with ease and purpose.

- Soul-declutter - take time, if you haven't done so already, to declutter your heart, mind and soul by taking 15 minutes to "rest" and be with God.

- Take a "Before" photo of the space you want to organize.

- Journal about any apprehensions or anxieties that came up in the visualization exercise.

BONUS: Bring your dreams to life! Make a collage or create a Pinterest board to give a visual to the space you envisioned!

ADDITIONAL RESOURCE: Are you a visual or auditory learner? Check out my six-week Reclaim Your Space with G.R.A.C.E. online course that includes a video lesson for each of the six weeks (melindagrace. com/course). Use it as a companion tool to take your organizing to the next level!

10 WAYS TO DECLUTTER THE SOUL

Whenever my soul, heart and mind feel full and distracted, I do a couple of the decluttering ideas on my list below. In fact, I unsubscribed from a few emails the other day in order to create more time and room in my mind for a specific life dream my husband and I are working on.

1. Turn off music or podcasts when you drive.
2. Go for a walk and listen to nature.
3. Unsubscribe from 3 e-mails.
4. Stick your toes in the sand.
5. Get a good night's rest—7-8 hours of sleep.
6. Breathe in 3 slow breaths.
7. Meditate for 15 minutes.
8. Unfollow a podcast.
9. Journal with no inhibitions.
10. Read the Bible.

WEEK TWO

GATHER

"Good planning and hard work lead to prosperity,
but hasty shortcuts lead to poverty."

Proverbs 21:5 (NLT)

We are ready to begin reclaiming our space by working through the organizing process! The first step in the acrostic **G.R.A.C.E.** is to **GATHER**.

I love this part of the process! It's time to get down to the nitty-gritty and get this party started! I warn you that *GATHERING*, at first glance, appears to be creating more chaos, not less. But trust me! When we expose the chaos, we can then begin to make wise decisions and set up systems that lead to structure.

In this first step, we are *GATHERING* and planting seeds for our success. We are going to *GATHER* three things: 1) Goals, 2) Organizations, and 3) Items. "Good planning and hard work lead to prosperity, but hasty shortcuts lead to poverty" (Proverbs 21:5 NLT). As we gather these things, we are giving ourselves the ability to assess the totality of the situation.

Recently, I zeroed in on organizing my kitchen spices. I started by pulling out ALL the spices and placing them on my kitchen table, sorting them in alphabetical order as I went. This allowed me to see duplicates and exactly how much of each spice I truly had. My husband and I married older in life, so between us, we had way too much! Many of them had lost their beautiful aromas and were no longer needed. I would not have been able to come to these conclusions without physically seeing all the spices together and sorted. That's what we are doing in this step—giving ourselves an accurate picture of all the objects for which we need to make decisions.

Let the journey from chaos to calm commence!

FACT

"Setting good goals starts with specificity."

George T. Doran[15]

GATHER

STEP ONE: GATHER your *GOALS*

I must confess. I LOVE setting goals! I love sitting in my vintage velvet green chair that I've had in my room since I was child and dreaming up all that could be. I often have more goals than anyone could achieve in a lifetime. Personally, I like to give myself time to dream up all that could be possible with a space! Take a minute to remember what you envisioned for your space in the last chapter. What did your space look like? Feel like? Smell like?

OK, back to goal setting! Let's make sure we're being **SMART** with our goals. The **S.M.A.R.T.** goals acronym was created by George T. Doran in 1981 and stands for **S**pecific, **M**easurable, **A**chievable, **R**ealistic, and **T**ime-bound.[16] This is an organizing book, not a goal setting book, so I'll keep this section brief.

Take some time to *GATHER* three goals for the space you are reclaiming. BE CAREFUL to set realistic goals that will allow you to walk through the process and complete them in the time you have available to you. You can always return to the steps and choose more detailed and challenging goals; but for now, to build your confidence, let's focus on something manageable!

Why start with goal setting? Because like Zig Ziglar says, "A goal properly set is halfway reached."[17] Psychology shows us that setting a goal can lead to increased motivation and success, and I want you to be SUCCESSFUL in your organizing journey. Tony Robbins (you've heard of him, right?) said, "Setting goals is the first step from turning the invisible to visible." [18]

Here's how it works: my vision for my office bookshelves is to create a sense of order, education, and whimsy. My word for this area of my home office is actually "SMART." How do I reach this vision for my space? By setting three goals for the space:

1. Go through ALL of the paper clutter and sort into categories: "To Shred" and "To Digitize" by April 24th.

2. Create zones for business, hobbies, and memories, and label accordingly by May 1st.

3. Add a touch of style and design that is whimsical, fun, and inspiring by May 8th.

Take some time now to set goals for your space that are **S.M.A.R.T.** Give each goal a due date. Write them down in your journal, on a scrap piece of paper, on your dry erase board, wherever, and then add them to your calendar on the day you want them to be completed by. If you're new to goal setting, I've included a list of recommended goal setting resources on my website, www.melindagrace.com/grace. Of course, my favorite is Zig Ziglar!

As you set goals for the space you want to organize, first and foremost consider the function of the room. How do you use the room currently? Think through all of the activities you do in that space. Does that work for you and your family? If not, how do you want the space to function? Feel free to dream here! Today we can literally hack any space to be used in a way that suits our needs and lifestyle. Setting this goal upfront will set you up for success in the long run, because when you know the function of the space, you also know what items live in the space.

I've been working with a wonderful lady, Samantha, for a few months on several areas of her home. She's a boss lady who owns and runs her own business, networks like crazy, and loves to have people over. We've been working on systems and decluttering so she can have people over again and not feel embarrassed.

Fall is in the air and Thanksgiving is quickly approaching. She wants to have friends stay with her for the holidays, but there's nowhere for them, except a room that is filled to the brim with stuff. A room once used as a bedroom is now functioning as a storage unit, linen closet, antique shop, and luggage haven. With only a few weeks until Thanksgiving, Samantha must make some decisions fast.

Together, we decide this will officially become a guest bedroom. Guest bedrooms are also great places to store less needed items that are used once or twice a year, so we select categories that she would like to store in this room and then everything else must either be decluttered or go elsewhere. The room has two closets. One will be for storing linens needed for this room only. The other is for gifts and gift wrapping. The dresser is for family photos, so she can easily access and reminisce with her friends and family over the holidays. Now we know the functions.

Everything else must find a new home. Period. Luckily, underneath all the clutter is a bed, dresser, and nightstand. So, the room functioning as a guest bedroom is easy. Antiques that are chosen to stay are moved to an area of the home where we've been gathering them to later determine if she should keep or sell. Kitchen appliances are donated because if they made it in here, they aren't being used in the actual kitchen. Luggage and anything travel related, we move to the garage, where we've already created an easy-to-access "Travel" zone.

The function of this room changed from a storage area to a functional guest bedroom with certain zones for specific categories of storage. Samantha is relieved. She can find fresh linens to make the bed for her friends arriving in a few days. She can also host them without tripping over clutter. Now that's something to be thankful for!

STEP TWO: GATHER your *ORGANIZATIONS*

As part of your decluttering project, you will naturally accumulate items to discard. The question becomes, "Where do I take these items?"

What top three *ORGANIZATIONS* would you consider using for your discarded items? Consider charities that will give you a receipt for tax write-offs. Consider resale shops (digital and storefronts) and local "free" groups on social media.

Pro-tip: Make sure the organizations you choose are on your "route" or a short distance off your normal driving routine; otherwise, the items will just sit in your car or garage! You can always ask a friend or relative to help you with drop-offs. Many donation centers also offer free pick-up services. In fact, I tried one out the other day, and it was so easy! I logged on to the non-profit's website, entered in my information, selected a date, and they showed up and took all my boxes away! EASY PEASY!

As you donate, sell, or give your items to a neighbor, you are keeping the "circular economy" going. WAIT! TIME OUT! What is a circular economy? According to Wikipedia, it is "a model of production and consumption, which involves sharing, leasing, reusing, repairing, refurbishing and recycling existing materials and products as long as possible."[19]

If you'd like to sell some of your items, then make sure to include at least one place to sell to on your list of top three organizations. I made over $1,000 one year selling my unwanted items on a social media platform. It took me all year and was a hassle, but patience is a virtue and I needed the cash! Note that selling items can be a slower process and more time-consuming than simply dropping them off at a charity. Consider the cost value for you and if you have the time to do it. For me, often the payoff is not in the money, but in knowing it's going to an actual person who wanted that particular item. Consider selling clothing (still in good condition) online or via apps on your phone. The simpler, the better!

If you need to get rid of an item in a hurry, listing that item on your online selling platform or app for $0 is a great way to attract interest. In my experience, the item is often gone within a day or two.

If you have not heard of them, consider your local **Buy Nothing Group** by the Buy Nothing Project. They recently launched an app, so if you're not on social media, don't despair! Their website explains: "The Buy Nothing Project is the world's biggest gift economy, being used in communities around the world, allowing neighbors to share freely with one another. What is a gift economy? It means everything shared on Buy Nothing is given freely, no money, no barter, no strings. Free."[20]

Consider if your items need to be recycled! Be sure to check your city and county websites for legal requirements on how to handle hazardous waste. They usually offer free services. For example, in Los Angeles, we have recycling centers that are open on the weekends for individuals to drop off e-waste like old TVs, printers, computers, batteries, paint, and other hazardous materials.

Take some time now in your journal to jot down ideas, and do a quick internet search of organizations and apps with missions you believe in that are near you, or that have an easy online process.

If you want more resources on charities, recycling, and selling online, I've created "Donation," "Recycle," and "Sell" guides that will give a great starting point. Go to melindagrace.com/resources.

STEP THREE: GATHER your *ITEMS*

Here's where we get to the FUN stuff!!!

First, we're going to GATHER sorting bins, sticky notes, and a permanent marker! For the bins, you can use boxes, plastic bins, or trash bags. Label them: KEEP, DONATE, TRASH, SELL, RECYCLE. You may even come across items that need to be given to a friend or family member. Simply create a "TO DO" bin, and put it by your door or workstation, so you can see what needs to leave the space but not get lost again.

On rare occasions, you will come across an item that you will have no idea where it should go, much less if you should keep it. Sometimes you need a minute (or two) to figure this out. But we don't want to slow the momentum you have going, so take a cue from my niece who also loves to organize. She was organizing her toys and came across some that didn't fit any of the categories she had bins for. She didn't know what to do with them, so she created a bin called "I DON'T KNOW." I love this! I find when I use this with my clients, it immediately relieves stress, and they can stay on task. By the time we loop back to this bin, they've already solved the problem of what to do with the items.

Next, we are going to *GATHER* all the items in the space you want to organize by pulling everything out. Yep. You heard me EVERYTHING! I know this seems very tedious and time-consuming (it is), but I can't tell you how much it makes a difference in the whole process. I recommend starting with a category. If, for example, you're organizing your bedroom, start with gathering every single item of clothing. Think through: are there other areas of my home or office where similar items are being stored? Bring out those items, too. Sort "like with like." This helps to see duplicates. In our bedroom example, this would be socks with socks, sleepwear with sleepwear, dresses with dresses, etc. In my kitchen example, I'm focused on my spices, so I will gather all my spices and alphabetize them so I can see any duplicates and then either keep them alphabetized or sort them into categories.

 **Pro-Tip:** If you have the room, create a "staging area" where you can see everything, and start to group and categorize items. If you don't have the space, pull things out in sections to still create a staging area, even if it's just the kitchen table.

If you're having trouble deciding where to start in the space you've decided to work on, there are a couple of ways to tackle this. You can start with what is stressing you out the most, so that you can see and feel immediate progress. Or you may want to start with an area that simply feels logical to you—maybe one that will clear a space that can then be used as the staging area for the next zone you will gather. Or consider working from one end of the room to the other.

There are many professional opinions on this and master organizers who have methods with very specific orders. One of the biggest lessons I learned from my acting days is to "start where you're stuck!" I truly live by that when I'm panicked or am simply repeating to myself, "I don't know. I don't know! Pause. "YES, I do know! I'm going to start where I'm stuck." The answers often reveal themselves, especially if you're relying on God's grace to get you through this process. We often hear His voice when we've come to the end of ourselves. We are creative beings, and while the general organizing process might be the same for everyone, there is room for your creativity. For your spark. Remember, "For I can do everything through Christ, who gives me strength" (Philippians 4:13 NLT).

Most clients come to me with a certain room they are ready to declutter and organize. Sometimes there is an organizing project with several rooms, and clients won't know where to start. They will show me all the areas and then look at me in complete overwhelm and ask, "Where do you think we should start?"

Like Sandra. She hired me after a recent move and wanted several rooms organized for her sanity. She was a single mom and full-time professor at a law school. After showing me the entire home, I asked her,

"Where do you want to start?" She gave me a blank stare. I inquired, "Is there an area that is bugging you the most?" "Yes!" she exclaimed, "The kitchen. I can't find anything. The holidays are coming, and my mother is coming over."

It was the area of her home that was immediately the most important and equally the most dysfunctional. I knew right away that the kitchen was indeed the heart of her new home, and if I could get the kitchen unpacked, decluttered, and organized, most of her stress would calm down. She was stuck. Stuck in her head and her heart about this new kitchen. She agreed, and I got to work right away.

Within a couple of sessions, her kitchen was totally unpacked, everything put away, with a home for every item. I noticed that as I picked up momentum, she did too! Every session, she'd show me what she did in-between our meetings. That kitchen had a ripple effect, and she knew immediately what to work on next. Could we have started somewhere else? Sure. But by starting where she was stuck, I tapped into her biggest pain point and was able to relieve it almost as fast as Tylenol!

You know. Your gut knows. Start where you're stuck.

PRAYER

1. Lord, be with me as I GATHER my goals and set my intentions. Let them conform to your will. Lead me down a path that opens up opportunities for me to hear your voice, serve my family and community with clarity, and love all who come across my path. "Good planning and hard work lead to prosperity, but hasty shortcuts lead to poverty" (Proverbs 21:5 NLT).

2. Lord, I also ask that you'd be with me as I GATHER the organizations and/or people you'd have me pass my things along to. Guide my thoughts and research to use the giving away or selling of these items to bless someone else on their journey. I ask for you to connect my unwanted items with those who want and need them. "If you need wisdom, ask our generous God, and he will give it to you" (James 1:5 NLT).

3. Jesus, I confess I need your strength to help me GATHER all my items in the area I'm working on. Give me wisdom to sort and categorize in a way that is useful and will show me all the physical blessings you've given to me. Show me where to start and remind me of all the places I have stored things and forgotten about them. "For I can do everything through Christ, who gives me strength" (Philippians 4:13 NLT).

REFLECT

Journal. Take a few minutes to journal about how you felt before starting this phase of the process. Then journal how you feel after you've gathered your items. Notice if any emotions come up. Take note. Pause and reflect on them.

DEEP DIVE

GATHER! Take all the time you need to literally gather and sort your:

- Goals

- Organizations

- All the items in the space you are organizing.

KITCHEN

The kitchen is one my favorite rooms to organize—and also the hardest. I think the kitchen is one of the best places to start because it is the heart of the home and where you'll find immediate relief and calm. It can be a bit tricky to organize because it's so personal and used by several people with several functions and zones. Here are 10 things you can declutter and release today. You can download more "Kitchen" resources at melindagrace.com/grace.

1. Spices that have lost their fragrance

2. Small appliances bought with good intentions but never used

3. Broken or damaged tools, utensils, gadgets, pots & pans

4. Plastic that you've used in the microwave or dishwasher—get rid of harmful toxins

5. Multiples where you only need one

6. Dirty or never used reusable bags

7. China or glassware given to you that you'll never use (It's OK. I promise.)

8. Never used cookbooks & recipe printouts

9. Food storage containers with no lid, or lids with no container

10. Food you won't use or has gone bad

WEEK THREE

RELEASE

"For everything there is a season, a time for every activity under heaven . . . A time to search and a time to quit searching; A time to keep and time to throw away."

Ecclesiastes 3:1, 6 (NLT)

As we go through your items, we're going to focus on *RELEASING* three specific things: **perfectionism**, **power**, and **particular items** that need to be let go.

I recently noticed that although I have a new, beautiful home office, I was choosing daily to work at my kitchen table instead. My husband often teased me about this, and I began to wonder why I was indeed not working in my office. What was this all about? Curious, I started an investigation. As I studied my office bookshelves, I saw a stack of journals that were filled with unhappy memories from my school days and memories from my struggling days as an actress. It occurred to me that the journals contained years of life and pain, anthems of longing for love, prayers for healing, and callings to childhood dreams. They represented my past insecurities; and now in my 40s, it was time to let them go.

So, I asked my husband for his advice, and he casually said, "We can burn them! It will be fun!" I was shocked at his quick and easy response. It made me bust out laughing. He's so rugged! Then, I sat on that idea for months. I was afraid I would lose myself if I truly let go of the journals.

Then, one night, we put my old journals in our fireplace and burned them together. It was a surreal experience. I was standing there with my husband, whom I had prayed for, for 20+ years. My heart was full of gratitude that God answered some of the prayers and equally thankful for the ones He didn't. I was thankful for how He'd carried me to this beautiful moment. I said goodbye to that insecure, hurt, anxiety-ridden, perfectionistic, people-pleasing girl. And I welcomed a new, confident, calm, God-trusting woman. I cried! Now when I enter my office, that strange, underlying burden on my soul isn't there. I finally feel focused and ready to achieve the purposes God has laid on my heart.

Not every "letting go" of our items is quite this dramatic or intense. Most of it will be easy and FUN! But my story is significant because it brings to light three lessons: 1) Releasing sometimes invokes intense and emotional experiences; 2) Releasing sometimes requires help and assistance; 3) Releasing sometimes takes time.

NOW is your time to keep or release!

FACT

"At its deepest level, the prospect of letting go forces us up against our three strongest emotional drivers: love, fear, and rage."

Judith Sills, Ph.D.[21]

ESSENTIAL

RELEASING is a very important act in both the renewal and restoration processes. Charles Swindoll reminds us, "Renewal and restoration are not luxuries. They are essential." [22] They are essential to leading a healthy and whole life and, strangely enough, can be the result of organizing our homes and offices. In keeping with our gardening theme, we are cutting and pruning the branches of "stuff" while at the same time allowing our Father to prune us and our spiritual branches. "I am the true grapevine, and my Father is the gardener. He cuts off every branch of mine that doesn't produce fruit, and he prunes the branches that do bear fruit so they will produce even more [. . .] Yes, I am the vine; you are the branches. Those who remain in me, and I in them, will produce much fruit" (John 15:1, 5 NLT).

You may feel the pruning as you *RELEASE* and let go of branches that are dead or cluttering up your physical space as well as your soul. It's not always a pleasant feeling, but the result is a beautiful vine full of amazing fruit!

STEP ONE: RELEASE your *PERFECTIONISM*

"For freedom, Christ set us free. Stand firm then and don't submit again to a yoke of slavery" (Galatians 5:1 CSB).

For most of my 20s and 30s, I pursued acting in hopes it would become my career. When I moved to Los Angeles, I also became a writer. My friends who were writers in Hollywood would say, "Done is better than perfect." When I was writing my solo show, I often found myself repeating that mantra to myself. That solo show was sold out at the 2018 Hollywood Fringe Festival and received rave reviews from fans and industry reviewers. That would not have happened if I didn't let go of perfectionism and simply write the show and finish it.

For our purposes, we need to release the idea of the "perfect" house, room, closet, etc. My husband and I recently moved and have been renovating our house. I'm constantly releasing the idea of the "perfect" home. It is so much fun to design and add style. It is a very joyful process, but it can quickly become frustrating and overwhelming when I put the emphasis on the result being perfect—which begs the question, perfect for whom? For that social media account with a million followers? For that favorite home and design magazine cover? For that one long lost friend who I'll never see again?

Perfectionism is focused on the self—fulfilling an insecurity from the past or about the future. *RELEASE* it! You don't need that in your life. Julia Cameron explains, "Perfectionism is a refusal to let yourself move ahead. It is a loop—an obsessive, debilitating closed system that causes you to get stuck in the details of what you are writing and to lose sight of the whole." [23] We're working towards putting our thoughts on something higher than ourselves and creating spaces that allow us to do so. So, give that to God. Let Him help you step out of perfectionism and into peace.

While it is fun to aim for that social media or magazine image you love of that "perfect" space, I want to add some perspective. That image is often staged by multiple people, with professional lighting, and captured and edited by a professional photographer and/or digital marketing expert. It takes money and a village to create the masterpieces you see online and in magazines, and at this point, you might be going solo with limited resources. Don't worry! *RELEASE* it. I promise you, using social media and magazines for inspiration ONLY, and then doing what is in your means and letting go of the rest, will still bring about a peace and joy that will surprise you and make you feel good!

The goal for me when organizing a client's house is to find—truly—what works for them, even if it's not worthy of the latest social media platform. What's more important to me is the way they "feel" in that space and that they can move into or access more fully who God created them to be.

A great example is one of my very first clients in Los Angeles during the global pandemic. We worked on her bookshelf together, decluttering it and choosing only the items that were meaningful to her. The result was perfect for her! It showcased her iPod from the 2000's, an exposed cord, pens and pencils that weren't organized by color. But you know what? This client had NO MONEY to spend on style and design; that old iPod made her extremely happy, and the bookshelf was 100% functional for her. She can find what she needs, it contains memorabilia that makes her happy, and it's way less cluttered than before we worked together!

STEP TWO: RELEASE your *PRIDE*

"For I can do everything through Christ, who gives me strength" (Philippians 4:13 NLT).

My mission is to help you find a sense of ease and confidence in your organizing journey. I believe a great source of inspiration and hope can be found when you let go of your pride and rely on Jesus' strength, the Holy Spirit's wisdom, and the support of community.

There is a lot teaching out there today about putting all your trust and strength in yourself alone. There are many teachers and business empires whose focus is to create such a high-energy, strong belief that "YOU can do everything." People flock to them en masse and spend thousands of their hard-earned dollars to build THEMSELVES up. This can be an expensive, exhausting, anxiety-ridden way to accomplish your purpose in life. Why go it alone? Who doesn't want some help? I want to encourage you that your savior, JESUS, can do everything—and He's FREE—absolutely no money necessary or required! In HIM you can do all things. You can *RELEASE* your pride and trust Him.

In my personal experience, it can induce anxiety when we tap into ONLY our own human power to build ourselves up to be courageous, vulnerable, smart, and wise. Jesus encourages us to remain "in Him." Pastor Ryan Rush warns us that "Believing in your own power will leave you miserable in the long term.⁴" For me, trusting in myself only to make all of my dreams come true and doing "all the things" without checking it with God's word led me to the lowest point in my life. Rather than leading me to peace and tranquility, my pride left me broken. Luckily, grace was there as Jesus' called to me: "Rejoice in the Lord always. I will say it again: Rejoice! Let your gentleness be evident to all. The Lord is near. Do not be anxious about anything, but in every situation, by prayer and petition, with thanksgiving, present your requests to God. And the peace of God, which transcends all understanding, will guard your hearts and minds in Christ Jesus" (Philippians 4:4-7 NIV). He has all of the power in the universe, and He wants to give YOU what you need. Let Him.

"In their hearts humans plan their course, but the **Lord** (emphasis mine) establishes their steps" (Proverbs 16:9 NIV). *RELEASE* the idea that you must do it all by yourself! God will give you direction and often friends, family, and other resources to help on the journey. There are helpful books, blogs, pictures, and videos all available with a quick internet search or online order. Even your local library has organizing books you can check out for free! Family and friends can be a great source of sound judgment, accountability, and support. I was in Houston for a month, spending time with family and going through my childhood stuff, when I had to stop and ask my sister for help. I asked her for answers to the questions I couldn't in that moment answer for myself. Her assistance was extremely valuable in helping me release items that no longer served me. It's funny how sometimes we just need permission from someone else to tell us that it's OK to let that item go.

Jasmine reached out to me after having tried to organize her kitchen on her own. She lived in an apartment with a tiny kitchen that could pack a clutter punch! Jasmine is a smart, successful businesswoman with a creative flare and passion for cooking delicious cuisine and hosting fabulous dinner parties. The problem: her kitchen is complete chaos, she can't find anything, she won't have anyone over, and this frustrates her.

Jasmine has tried on her own. Been there, done that, and bought the organizing product as a souvenir. She finally had to admit that she couldn't do it without help and brought me on board. Which is great, because I LOVE organizing kitchens. I followed the process you're learning in this book and coached her along the way. The kitchen is functional now. She can find things. Most importantly, she's not embarrassed and has since hosted dinner parties galore—changes made by simply asking for help.

If she can ask for help, you can too!

STEP THREE: RELEASE your *PHYSICAL ITEMS*

Here is where you will physically go through each item one by one and make decisions—keep, toss, donate, sell, recycle. For some, this part is easy and you will want to touch each individual item and decide if it stays or goes. But, if you are dealing with more sentimental items, it may be easier if someone else holds the object for you. Keep in mind that often there is what is called "kinesthetic sympathy" at play. According to Wikipedia, "Kinesthetic sympathy is the state of having an emotional attachment to an object when it is in hand which one does not have when it is out of sight."[24] You can ask yourself this question: "Does the item offer up grace?" Keep items that offer you a sense of grace, love, and usefulness. Keep in mind that you may not love your hammer, but you use it, so keep it!

Here's a set of reasons to release an item:

- Not used in a year

- You don't LOVE it

- It's broken and you don't want to or have the time to fix it

- It doesn't fit

- There are weird, unwanted, negative, or uncomfortable feelings physically or emotionally

For most of my clients, this is the part of the process they can't do on their own, which is why they've hired me. Take Maria for example. Her house is beautiful, gorgeously decorated and bordering on minimalism. Her closet, however, was a source of frustration and embarrassment. Pushing past her pride, she allowed me into her closet, where a few items of clothing were on the floor, a few, full small bags of contents that she had no idea about, and a couple of random items in random places. In all honesty, it was not very much stuff and you may be thinking why did she call me in the first place? Because she couldn't do it on her own.

For many people, it's hard to focus on sorting, categorizing, and making decisions. That day, I held space for her to be present, to tell me the stories, to let out her anxiety, to talk through the decisions with her, and to be her cheerleader. She always works alongside me and has no difficulty making decisions once I'm there. During this session, she actually found her long-lost passport in a bag she went through while I was going through another bag. Together we went through everything in her closet. Maybe you need a friend or family member to hold space for you while you make decisions and release items. You've released your pride, so what are you waiting for? Text them now to come over!

WHY IS IT HARD TO RELEASE?

If you are finding it hard to release a particular item or, in general, letting things go, realize you are not alone! We become emotionally attached to our stuff, and we are often coming face to face with ourselves—past, present, and future. Each item we hold unlocks memories from seasons or events in our lives filled with past and/or current relationships. Sometimes it's a joy and other times it's overwhelming to confront ourselves and our memories—and at the same time, decide what to do with them in a moment. You are brave!

Chaplain Kevin Deegan teaches in his workshop on "Mental Wellness" that with any change, there's a loss.[25] Even in letting go of items, there is a loss. You are physically losing the item and, in many instances, you are losing and letting go of an emotion, memory, or experience that has been living with you in that space for years.

If this happens during the releasing phase, I recommend taking a minute to sit with the item, and as Chaplain Kevin encourages, "Recognize and accept the loss you will feel from letting it go." You may want to consider taking a photo of the item to help you release it. Then, thank God for the item and how it has blessed your life and how He provided it when you needed it. This part of the organizing process may have just become a bit harder than you thought. Lysa Terkeurst reminds us, "If there was ever a secret for unleashing God's powerful peace in a situation, it's developing a heart of true thanksgiving."[26] Don't forget the power of simply giving thanks to the Lord. Then, ask Him to show you how to discard it and if there's anyone else that could benefit from the item.

Here are some additional questions to ask that might help:

- Is there anything spiritual or emotional that needs to be released along with the item?

- Are there any attitudes or negative thoughts that go hand in hand with this item that do not align with what God says about you?

For YEARS, I kept my high school prom dress in my closet. It lived with me in several apartments, and I don't honestly know why, because although it was pretty and reminiscent of Kate Winslet's style in the movie *Titanic*, I did not have the best time at my prom! It was not a good experience for me, except for the salmon I had at dinner. I hate to say it, but I just now, this year, donated the dress to a Girl Scout who was gathering formals for high schoolers who could not afford one. Luckily for me, the '90s are back in fashion. *Phew!* I am no longer holding onto any negative thoughts or disappointment I felt for not having a great prom experience.

Maybe you need to *RELEASE* guilt and forgive yourself. "As far as the east is from the west, so far has He removed our transgressions from us" (Psalm 103:12 NKJV). Many of my older clients feel guilt for wanting to part with heirlooms or items passed down to them by a loved one. It really is difficult for them, and they carry this weight of guilt or the fear of the guilt they will have if they part with these items. It truly is OK to let go and release any current or future guilt. That item served your loved one, and now it's time for the item to find a new service assignment other than you—guilt-free.

This is a lot to take in, and sometimes we are not mentally in a healthy place to do so. You may need to call in a Professional Organizer, a friend, a counselor, or coach to help you process any emotional or spiritual weeds and thorns tied to your items. Let me remind you, again, that it's totally OK to ask for help! I had a client that was going through her closet clothes and was doing great! She was making quick decisions, and we were having a grand 'ole time. Until we came across a beautiful white nightgown that she had received as a wedding gift. Momentum completely shifted gears and halted to a standstill. She explained that what was supposed to be a joyful gift was indeed not and that it had a negative memory associated with it that brought up pain and sadness. It was a high-end, never-been-worn, tags-still-on gorgeous silk nightgown. I held space for her in that moment, to receive the memories it brought up and to accept that it was OK to release the item without guilt. Together we came up with a solution to sell it on Poshmark—and it sold within a few weeks! Sometimes all you need is someone to come stand in the gap for you.

WHAT IF I NEED IT AGAIN?

"What if I need it again?" This question does come up from time to time when decluttering. And the culprit, I believe, is a scarcity mindset. A scarcity mindset is when you laser focus on something you can't have or, in this case, can't have again because of an unmet need like time or money. It is crazy the number of times I've had this thought while decluttering, reminded myself of how God always provides, given something away to a friend or charity, and then when I needed something similar, it was there for me—and often better than the version I had released.

An antidote to a scarcity mindset is contentment. Contentment is "feeling or showing satisfaction with one's possessions, status or situation."[27] The Bible teaches us that "true godliness with contentment is itself great wealth. After all, we brought nothing with us when we came into the world, and we can't take anything with us when we leave it" (1 Timothy 6:6-7 NLT). To me, contentment is a concept that I have to feel, and it's often nebulous. One way I've found to grow the contentment muscle is to practice gratitude.

Gratitude is an appreciation for receiving something from someone else. We all have an abundance, and it's OK to be grateful to God for what He's given you. You may look at this pile of items you're releasing and think, *What if I need it again?* Instead, look at all the items you've chosen to keep and let gratitude sweep over you. Dietrich Bonhoeffer reminds us that, "It is only with gratitude that life becomes rich!"[28] Even in decluttering, we can pause for a minute and give an offering to God of gratitude. This offering can help us get back on track with our organizing goals and also make the process more peaceful and calm. I love this quote by A.W. Tozer: "Gratitude is an offering precious in the sight of God, and it is one that the poorest of us can make and be not poorer but richer for having made it."[29]

I always feel more connected to God when my heart is full of thanks, but did you know there are also health benefits to gratitude?

Actual scientific research shows that gratitude practiced regularly can lower levels of depression, reduce anxiety, decrease the risk of heart disease, and lower blood pressure! It can improve relaxation and sleep and also relieve stress.[30] When we stop to organize and deal with our clutter and the questions that arise with gratitude, we can experience symptoms of improved health!

DECLUTTER

We finally get to use those sorting bins we gathered in Week 2!!! *Woohoo*! As you go through your items, take the time to put the released items in their respective bins or bags: Keep, Donate, Recycle, Sell, and Trash.

 **Pro-Tip:** Create as many bins, bags, or boxes as you need for the items that don't belong in this space. Other bin ideas include, "I Don't Know," "To Fix," "Goes in Another Room," and "Outgoing" (meaning the item leaves your house to be mailed, given to a friend, taken to work, etc.).

Now is the time to take the items to your charity of choice, to the recycling center, or post them online. At the very least, move the donation box to your car. This will give you an immediate feeling of accomplishment, and you will start to feel the energy shifting in your home and in your spirit.

I want to encourage you that it's OK if the reviewing and releasing part takes longer than you would think. It is a muscle that needs to be developed, a mindset that can take some time to shift. Some items you might not be ready to even go through, while others you need another few months to get used to the idea of letting it go. And you know what? It's alright. When this happens, I simply create a bin of items to review at a later date and store it in area that isn't prime real estate in my home.

Stephanie and I have been working together for about a year. She's downsizing from a large house to a one-bedroom ADU, and it's hard. I go at her pace during our sessions. Often times, items she was not ready to let go of during one decluttering session, she's ready to release by the next session a few months later with no problems at all. Sometimes during our sessions we'll come across photos, VHS tapes, DVDs, and slides that take a lot of time, memory, and emotion to declutter and organize. So, I simply group them together, put them in bins, and store them all in one area for us to review at a later date when she has the capacity to look through them and make decisions. Guess what? She's almost there! I've taught her the importance of digitizing media that is decaying literally every day and, in a couple of months, we're going to sort out the items she wants to digitize, which will be a lot easier now that we have all the media items stored in one place.

It doesn't always have to be as fast as you see on TV shows. Remember, there's room for grace. However, once you get the hang of it and experience how good it feels to declutter, you'll speed up in no time. I have two clients right now that are in a competition to be the fastest decision-maker. They go so fast with making decisions that I can't keep up! Donate, Goes in Another Room, Keep, Recycle, Goes to a Friend—they fly through their items while I run around moving them to their respective piles. It's a game, and it's fun.

PRAYER

"Heavenly Father, **I release** to You the burdens that I have been carrying, burdens that You never intended for me to carry. **I cast** all my cares upon You—all my worries, all my fears. You have told me to not be anxious about anything, but rather to bring everything to You in prayer with thankfulness.

Father, **calm** my restless spirit, **quiet** my anxious heart, **still** my troubling thoughts with the assurance that You are in control. I let go of my grip upon the things I have been hanging onto, with open hands I come to You. **I release** to Your will all that I am trying to manipulate; **I release** to Your authority all that I am trying to control. **I release** to Your timing all that I have been striving to make happen.

I thank You for Your promise to **sustain** me, **preserve** me, and **guard** all that I have entrusted to Your keeping. **Protect** my heart and mind with Your peace, the peace that passes all understanding. Father, may Your will be done in my life, in Your time, and in Your way."

— Roy Lessin,
Co-founder of DaySpring
(largest Christian greeting card company in the world)

REFLECT

Journal. Take a few minutes to journal about what you just read. Do you anticipate coming across any emotional clutter or obstacles while releasing your physical clutter? If so, take a moment to journal about who you can reach out to for help or what resources you can use to help you process the experience.

Write your own prayer of *RELEASE*.

DEEP DIVE

Practice. Go through all your sorted items and decide what needs to be released. Place those items into the respective bins you gathered and labeled. Reminder: this is a 6-week study, so lean into and focus on the process. You have one week to accomplish a lot. Stay the course! If anything gets too difficult, set it aside for another time.

Map it! Plan out when you will do your donation or recycling drop-offs or post items in an app and then do it.

Return it. Found items that don't belong in this area? Go ahead and return them to their proper home.

Journal. How'd it go?

BONUS: Ask a friend to come help you declutter and review, or turn on your favorite music or TV show!

PRIMARY CLOSET

I absolutely LOVE organizing closets! There are so many beautiful and functional things you can do in a closet. It's incredible. You can really organize your closet in a way that combines functionality and style more than any other room in the house and literally create a space for you to ENJOY it. Here are my Top 10 Favorite Ways to Organize a Closet. You can download more "Closet" resources at melindagrace.com/grace.

1. Release anything that makes you feel fat, doesn't fit, or brings up a bad memory

2. Create a box for memorabilia clothing to store up high

3. Acquire ALL MATCHING HANGERS—trust me on this one

4. Install a custom closet system to maximize space & efficiency

5. Create zones for dresses, shirts, pants, skirts, that match your rhythms of getting dressed

6. Hang clothes for how you would get dressed from top to bottom—tops on the top clothing bars, pants on the bottom

7. Mix 'n' match textures of bins in your aesthetic

8. Add pictures that mean something to you

9. Add beautiful things to display your jewelry and make you smile

10. LABEL

PHOTOS & MEMORABILIA

I love going through photos and memorabilia with my clients because I get to see photos of humans in all kinds of settings doing all kinds of things. It's so fun! Oftentimes going through these items, however, is not for fun reasons and mostly likely because of a life transition concerning a loved one. So, I encourage you to not wait until those emotional times in life to go through your own photos and memories. Start now! Personally, I tackle a piece every year. This year I plan to work with my sister on our '80s Barbie collection. What will you tackle this year? Here are some tips to help you release photos and memorabilia. You can download more "Photo" organizing resources at melindagrace.com/grace.

1. Just start

2. Gather all photos not in frames from all areas of your home into one area

3. Sort photos into general, chronological times of life on the first pass; get rid of duplicates and cringe-worthy pics

4. Second pass: get more specific with dates and events and decide which photos are "keep" worthy

5. Acquire acid-free photo boxes to store your "keep" photos

6. Digital photos: delete blurry, similar, or cringe-worthy photos; delete photos that hold bad memories or have people you don't know in them

7. Take breaks often & reward yourself— this is hard work

8. Don't be afraid to give away items for free; the feeling and story are often better than any money earned from selling

9. Take pictures of items that still have meaning but you are ready to release

10. Write down the memory associated with memorabilia and then release

WEEK FOUR

ACQUIRE

"A house is built by wisdom and becomes strong through good sense. Through knowledge its rooms are filled with all sorts of precious riches and valuables."

Proverbs 24:3-4 (NLT)

We are ready for the "A" in our G.R.A.C.E. acronym. "A" stands for **ACQUIRE**. In this step, we will *ACQUIRE* containers, bins, boxes, shelving, and other tools needed to contain our chosen items and give them a functional and beautiful home.

I LOVE this part of the organizing process because it allows us to be strategic and creative. To be clear, we need to acquire wisely and not go overboard. We must be careful to acquire items that support us in our new, organized lifestyle. What do we need in our spaces to tie everything together and contain our "riches" as in Proverbs 24:3-4?

I, personally, am a little "risk-averse" when it comes to acquiring organizing containers. It takes time to find the ones that are useful and that fit within my budget. I recently faced this when figuring out how to best organize my kitchen spices. After spending a great deal of time and energy researching online and in stores, I decided that storing my spices in a drawer was the best solution for the space. I ordered new glass jars with bamboo lids and pre-printed matching spice labels. All I had to do was peel and stick in place (my kind of DIY!). The result was a beautiful, purposefully sourced spice drawer with easy-to-read labels, and organized in a way that I can easily find and return my spices after I've used them.

ACQUIRING the right storage containers and accessories can empower you to keep clutter at bay without losing functionality. You've done the hard work of gathering and releasing your items; now, let's have fun and be creative!

FACT

Did you know that in The Container Store alone, there are over "10,000 innovative and multifunctional solutions designed to simplify customers' lives, save space and, ultimately, save time?" The Container Store[51]

ACQUIRE

Some simple tools you might need to acquire include a label maker, labels, label holders, post-it notes, pens, and sharpies. You might want to grab your tape measure now, too! It's worth taking the time to measure the shelf or drawer for which you want to acquire some bins to make sure they are the right size. If you are buying furniture or shelving, you will need to know the dimensions of the space you are working with. There's nothing worse than buying something too big or too small!

Also consider if you need any accessories for your space. For example, does your closet need some cedar planks or lavender to keep clothes fresh and keep the bugs away? Does your kitchen need drawer liners? Take a few minutes to assess everything you are keeping and the space(s) to which you plan to return the items. Also, think through your budget and stick with it. Once you see all the amazing storage options out there, you will want to overspend—trust me! Pace yourself and only acquire what you need to complete your current project. Seriously, there is a limit to bins and the problems they solve.

Creating a roadmap for the bins you want is a great exercise that will make the next step after this a lot easier. Not sure how to create your organizing roadmap? Here's how I do it: The first thing I like to do—because I love design and making spaces as beautiful as my clients and their budgets will allow me—is to create a private Pinterest board and label it the room or area I'm working on. Then I spend about 30 minutes to an hour looking through Pinterest for pictures, ideas, and inspiration that match the aesthetic and functionality I want for my client. I also play around on The Container Store website and scroll through Instagram taking screenshots of inspirational organizing designs and products. I then draw out the room (or closet or cupboard) on old school graph paper and write in my measurements. I create zones and map it all out on paper. Then, when all looks good and works, I move onto actual product selection.

Many products are linked within the social media sites themselves, so I click on the links and look up the product, the cost, the dimensions, and availability. I make a list of everything I want that will fit on the shelves or in the drawers with counts of each item with the price. I add it all up. Is this within my client's budget? If yes, I proceed and follow my roadmap. I order the product and have it on hand for the next session.

At this point you might be thinking, "Why do I need to put items in a bin anyway?" For many of us, not having specific homes for items can lead to a massive junk pile! When you give an item a bin, it now has a home and the clutter is contained. Bins also put a limit on what you should keep. They offer a gentle, physical reminder that if something doesn't fit into the properly placed bin, then you may have too much, and it may be time to discard something. This organizing rule is a great one to live by and that I encourage all my clients to implement: one in, one out!

A client I am working with has beautiful metal baskets to store her pillowcases, sheets, and blankets. The baskets are a cue to her that if she adds more pillowcases, she has more than she needs. She now has a gentle nudge to discard an old pillowcase that is perhaps stained or discolored. It can become a rag and move to a new home, thus creating a space for her new pillowcase. Clutter avoided!

I'd love to give you some helpful tips before you assess and ACQUIRE what you need!

 **Pro Tip:** Before you buy any organizing supplies, have a plan, purpose, and budget for the item(s). Otherwise, you may be adding to your clutter. The right bins, properly placed, help you create homes for items and cultivate new rhythms for putting things away quickly. However, just because you have fancy containers doesn't mean you are organized! They, too, can become part of the problem and chaos. They can turn into areas where we hide items we don't want to deal with. We don't want that!

I took on a huge organizing job at a church in Pasadena. At first glance, they appeared to be organized. I thought, "This job will be EASY! Everything is in bins and labeled. They just need some tidying and maybe better placement of the bins." WAS I WRONG!!! The bins were, in reality, hiding a mountain of clutter and trash. Nothing was in the correct storage container, and none of it made sense! Consequently, it took a few months to sort it all out. We re-used most of the bins, but also had to acquire new ones, especially for the craft supplies.

So, you see, our goal is not to purchase bins to hide our chaos and clutter; we are purposefully sourcing bins and storage containers that will house the items we have chosen to keep! We are being WISE, not frivolous!

 **Circular Economy Tip:** A great way to save money and contribute to a circular economy is to use what you already own. There are tons of DIY blogs and videos for how to use items like cardboard boxes, fabric scraps, and other common household items to use as bins. Many people are big fans of reusing shoe boxes for storage. With the plethora of shipping boxes out there, your ideas and solutions could be endless! Find your favorite DIY blogger, use your creativity, and have fun.

One of my first clients had a limited budget for product but wanted drawer dividers. So, I researched several DIY blogs and then, with the client's permission, used her favorite fabric scraps and some cardboard boxes. I measured her drawers, cut the cardboard into dividers, and covered them with fabric. Voila! Beautiful, custom drawer dividers!

 **Eco-Friendly Tip:** If you are concerned about the harmful effects of plastic on our bodies and our environment, consider purchasing items that are responsibly sourced and recyclable. Consider choosing plastic or paper bins that have been made from post-consumer recycled plastic and paper. When you are shopping for baskets, look for ones that are made from renewable resources. Containers made of bamboo, other types of wood and glass, can be a good alternative to plastic. There are more options coming on the market every year; and if you learn of something, please let me know—I'm on the journey with you! Most eco-friendly options are a bit more expensive, so plan your budget accordingly or acquire them used if necessary.

 **Budget-Conscious Tip:** Consider going to your local dollar store. My sister uses bins in her pantry that she bought for $1. They are fun colors, and they do the job just fine! Also consider shopping at the off-price retail shops, buying used online, or requesting a free bin or two from your local

social media "free" group. You'll be amazed at what you can find at a discount or even free! When my husband and I moved to our new home, we didn't have the budget for new storage items, so I stalked my new free online group and was "gifted" several awesome pantry storage bins that I use to this day! They saved me hundreds of dollars.

 **Designer Tip:** Here's where it gets really fun! Think about your style vs. functionality. Do you need clear bins so you can see what's inside? Do you want your kitchen aesthetic to be black and white, or your kid's room to be the colors of the rainbow? Do you want your items hidden and out of sight? Gather ideas from online and social media. Research the different price points, and don't forget to measure the space where the bins or baskets will go. Remember your budget, and let that be a boundary for you.

As I said, I LOVE organizing and styling closets! One of my favorite ways to add style for one client was to add pops of gold in a closet. Gold metal hat stands. Gold metal shoe stands. Gold label holders. This client loved a pop of glamour—and I had fun designing it.

The perfect example of this is Allie. Allie is an amazing photographer with a gorgeous studio space. She hired me to help her organize her studio office because it was driving her insane, and she wanted to be able to converse with her clients physically in that room from time to time. The state it was in now meant no client would see this room. Ever.

Allie's photography has a very specific look and aesthetic that people pay top dollar for. She, in a nutshell, has very specific branding, and her main goal for organizing her studio office was to do it in a way that matched her brand completely. I was as a giddy as a school girl! I love adding design to my organizing projects. I reviewed her website and photos to tap into the essence of Allie's brand. I researched and acquired bins, baskets, and other products that not only matched her brand but were functional. I even printed the labels for the bins and baskets in her business brand font!

The end result was a room that was beautiful AND functional. Allie was excited! Everything has a home. She has a system. And she has an on-brand, gorgeous office to host clients.

When you combine your new organizing dance with your beautiful style, a simpler life will unfold. When your system is in place, you will no longer need to figure out what to do with items or with the piles that happen, because you know where everything goes and you'll have fun putting it away in your bins that match who you are.

PRAYER

Lord, Jesus, thank you for all the resources you've given me to properly take care of the blessings you've given me! Guide me in proper planning of time, space, and money, and lead me to the people and places that will have what is needed to finish this step and create a "home" for the items chosen to live in my house. May each item be a blessing to me, my family, and all who enter my home. May they even be a source of inspiration to bless those around me! Give me wisdom in shaping my space so that it cultivates godliness and contentment. Amen. "But don't begin until you count the cost. For who would begin construction of a building without first calculating the cost to see if there is enough money to finish it?" (Luke 14:28 NLT).

REFLECT

Journal. In your journal, draw, collage, or list your ideas of items you'd like to ACQUIRE for your space. Have fun!

DEEP DIVE

Assess and *ACQUIRE*. Take a few minutes right now to assess everything you're keeping and the space(s) you will return the items to. Decide what bins and accessories you need for your newly organized spaces. Set your budget, and stick with it! Be careful NOT to overspend!!!

Pace yourself and only acquire what you need to complete your current project.

Decide if you need to hire a pro. This may be a great time to reach out to a handyman, a painter, or a closet company (if you are reimagining or redesigning your closet). Maybe you have a family member who is good at what you need done? Now is the time to give them a call! Many organizers bring in a professional for the more difficult construction-oriented projects, especially if spaces need to be created or used in a more efficient way.

BONUS: Do you need help finding a solution that fits your budget? Are you overwhelmed and don't know where to start? Pop on over to my website, melindagrace.com/grace. You will find examples of my favorite bins and uses for them. There, you will also find a checklist that you can download in case you get stuck or need more guidance.

GARAGE

The garage is where storage and items on their way out of your life merge into a jumbled mess, which can leave even the most organized frustrated and overwhelmed. My biggest tip for the garage is: Don't go it alone! Call a friend or family member. Of course, I'd love it if you called me. The garage is also a place for some of the most functional, yet coolest products to acquire. Here's my Top 10 list of must-have garage storage items. You can download more "Garage" resources at melindagrace.com/grace.

1. Matching weathertight storage bins that come in several sizes
2. Sturdy wire shelving
3. Custom cabinets or Elfa shelving
4. A heavy-duty rolling cabinet tool chest—in a color that matches, of course
5. A slatwall or peg board wall for sports equipment or gardening tools like brooms, rakes, etc.
6. Mounted overhead rack
7. Wall mounted hooks
8. Small, clear containers
9. Hydraulic lift overhead rack
10. LABELS

WEEK FIVE

CULTIVATE

"You have turned my mourning into joyful dancing."

Psalm 30:11 (NLT)

We are ready for the "C" in our G.R.A.C.E. acronym. "C" stands for **CULTIVATE**. In one of my favorite planners by Cultivate What Matters, they define *CULTIVATE*, "to break up the soil in preparation for new growth. To tend. To grow." We've already started to "break up the soil" in our homes or offices by pulling everything out, tending to the weeds, and discarding anything unnecessary, unhealthy, or not contributing to the person God wants us to be and become. Now it's time to "break up" old habits by putting everything back in place in such a way that it gives you more time, efficiency, and room to grow as a whole person.

In my home office, I'm in the process of cultivating an organizing system that not only helps me find things but enables me to be more efficient and productive. My office includes my desk with filing drawers, an armoire, and bookshelves with plenty of room for lots of items. Systems don't have to be complicated! My office desk has two filing drawers. One holds my personal files, and the other holds my business files. My armoire system is simple, too! The first shelf is for items I'm in the process of giving away, the second shelf for items I'm selling, and the third is for office supplies. One bookshelf holds my personal books and memorabilia, and the other displays my business books, inspiring items, and printer supplies. I make decisions about where to put things based on my rhythms and movement patterns in this space. It's my own little dance within my home office.

From last week's *ACQUIRE*, grab the new bins you purchased, or the awesome ones you just made, and begin the process of putting your items away. Carefully give each item its own home in your space. Consider how you use the item. What are the patterns and rhythms around how you find the item you need; where and how do you use the item, and how do you put it away? With these thoughts in mind, place your items in a way that supports this movement. Don't worry if it's right or wrong. This is your cultivated organizing system. Your dance.

FACT

"Dance is human behaviour composed of **purposeful, intentionally rhythmical** (emphasis mine), and culturally patterned sequences of nonverbal body movement . . ."

Judith Lynne Hanna, *The Performer-Audience Connection: Emotion to Metaphor in Dance and Society*[32]

DANCE

The goal is to be able to find what you need, when you need it, and to be able to put it away quickly. In the organizing world, we call this a system. To understand this abstract concept better, I liken it to a choreographed dance. When the dance is in motion, clutter will not have a chance to build back up again. This dance consists of practical, daily habits and movements that make a massive difference when everyone is on the "same beat." Like when you watch a dance performance, you can see when a dancer is off, or missed a step, or raised the wrong arm. And you know what they do when that happens? They keep going. They don't stop the whole performance because they missed a step. As theatre aficionados say, "The show must go on!"

The same is true in your house. The show must and will go on even if you miss a night of doing the dishes. So, give yourself grace as you learn new choreography or revive an old dance routine. Don't forget to turn on some music and have fun!

I really want you to craft a beautiful dance unique to you and your family, so here are some Pro Tips to help you cultivate your own rhythms:

 **Categorize:** We already mentioned categorizing when we gathered all of our items. At this point, "like" should be with "like." When you put your items away, do your best to keep them categorized and all together. This gives your brain less to think about when you need to find and use something. It lessens the old habit of buying duplicates and wasting money because you couldn't find something. For example, in my pantry I keep all the pastas together, the flours together, the nuts together, etc. You can categorize in a million different ways as long as it makes sense to you. This does take some discipline and time to figure out, so be patient.

 **Dance:** Create systems and rhythms that work for you. It's the combination of the natural rhythms of how you move and function in your space and the system with which you put items back in their place. This dance should make your life flow more efficiently. If your dance moves are off, you will know it! The clutter builds up.

At one point, my husband and I had a box by the door. This box held anything that needed to go out of the house, into our cars, and to their new homes. This was a system for us. Without this box, the reusable grocery bags would forever sit on the kitchen countertop and that coupon I needed for shopping would forever lie in the mail pile. My system may not work for you because it doesn't sync with your rhythms. That's OK! In fact, my husband and I no longer have a box by our door. Our choreography (rhythms) changed and yours will, too, over time.

 **New Choreography:** You may need to learn new routines. You may want to try that cool idea from a blog you read. You may even need the help of an organizer. A new set of moves may just be the thing you and your family need to get in sync—to find the rhythm that brings you together or brings clarity to your calling.

One of the reasons I love unpacking projects is because I get to create completely new choreography for my clients. They have a fresh start at learning new dance moves. One of my favorite unpacking jobs was for an inspiring lady who moved to a new home in Beverly Hills. She ran her own business and didn't have time to unpack and set up her new home. I brought in other organizers, and we tackled unpacking every box in every room. We made decisions and got her set up with new choreography in her new home.

She lived in it a few weeks and then had me back to refine the systems and organization to match the new rhythms she had found.

That's key: finding your rhythms and adjusting as needed.

 **In Sync:** When I organize clients, I ask them about their daily routines and how they currently use the space. Unless I see a more efficient way, I do my best to organize their items to match their current rhythms. If I change their system, I work with them to ensure they are in sync with the new way. It has to make sense to them, and it has to work for them. I strongly advise that you don't stray too far from what you currently do or the routines you naturally have with your space, unless it's completely not working or is unhealthy.

Closets are the spaces where I, more often than not, do challenge a client's existing system. Joan had a walk-in closet and brought me in to declutter, organize, and give her easy-to-maintain systems. I noticed right away that her jeans and pants lived tucked away on one side of the closet, her tops hung on the opposite side, and her shoes sprawled out everywhere. I took some time to chat with my client about how she moved in her space to determine which side of the closet she naturally gravitated towards to get dressed.

I then moved her pants and jeans to the bottom clothing rods and her tops right above them on the top clothing rods. I moved jackets to a nearby section and only kept the shoes she wore often on this side of the closet. I totally changed her dance and reviewed it with her to make sure she was in sync. She loved it. Now she only needed to go to one area of her closet to get dressed. Not much else changed. I only changed what was tripping up her rhythm.

 **Welcome Home:** Every single item must have a HOME! If you've followed any professional organizer in the last 40 years, you know this rule by now. It's the common thread in every organizer's work. Why? Because it's true! When your item doesn't have a home, it will go wherever, and clutter will build up. You won't deal with it because you don't know where it goes, and

you don't have time to figure it out. But good news: you have time NOW! You've devoted these six weeks to tackling this space at this moment. You will save yourself time and energy in the future. People meet me and are in awe of what I do. Their first question is always, "What's your biggest tip?" This is it! Everything must have a home! They shake their heads like, duh, I've heard this before! You have. You know it. Now do it!

Often, when you are putting things away and giving each item a home, you will come across items whose future home is uncertain. The category it belongs in is unclear, and you just don't know what to do with the item. Many times, when this happens, you will stick it in a drawer with no rhyme or reason and move on. But wait! This is how clutter builds back up. A little trick I do when this happens and I get stuck is to set the item aside for a minute. I don't put it away yet. I move onto other items that I know exactly where to put. It's honestly crazy how the answer reveals itself 100% of the time, and everything falls into place. A client will decide they no longer need that item, or a new space opens up that fits that item perfectly, or an idea of how to shift categories and rework a space leads to the unclear items now having a home. When this happens, I light up inside. It's as if it was always meant to be that way and I solved the riddle! You will, too.

One troublesome category that always comes up when I'm organizing is the "Project" category. Many items that end up as clutter are simply items that belong to incomplete projects. We're talking about craft projects, home renovation projects, photo and memorabilia projects, etc. As the desire to start or continue a project dangles in front of you while you're figuring out its new home, pause and be truthful with yourself. Will you really complete that project? How much space will the supplies take up? Do I need to go back to step two and RELEASE this project and all the items that go with it?

 **Be Vigilant:** As you live life, new items will come into your home, and that's OK. As you go about cultivating your new habits of organization and ease, be vigilant about allowing every new item to cross the threshold. If you do let it in, where will it live? Do you need to pause and create a space for that item? Is it worth taking up the cost of that square foot in your home? I'm originally from Houston, TX, but I currently live in Los Angeles, CA. As I write this book, the general average cost of a square foot of residential home in Houston is about $170. In Los Angeles, it's roughly $712!!! Every year when I go home for Christmas, I work diligently on decluttering my childhood through college items. When deciding whether to keep something and bring it back to Los Angeles, I ask myself, "Does this item mean that much to me that it's worth storing in a space that costs $712/sq. ft?!?!"

Another way you can be vigilant—which isn't very fun but very effective—is to refuse freebies. The free handouts at the mall, free flyers about the latest product you need (but really don't), the free pen with a company's business name on it, or free beauty sample that you will honestly never try. It's soooo fun to get free things, but the truth is, you don't need it! I confess, I often will give back the free gift given to me by a business or leave it on their vendor table. I really don't want extra clutter in my house and added advertising that clutters my brain. My biggest weakness is my Buy Nothing group. People post great stuff—for FREE! Even I have to be vigilant with myself. It's so hard. I only will ask to receive the free item if I truly think I will love it, have a home for it, and will use it or enjoy it . . . A LOT. If I can resist a beautiful, free teacup set, you can, too!

LABEL LOVE

Now is a good time to mention labels! Labeling bins, drawers, boxes, food containers, wires, etc. is the secret sauce to add to your organizing dance. Let's take off old, worn-out dance shoes and put on new, magical ones by removing all the packaging with advertising and extraneous legal jargon and adding simple, concise labels. This will clear space in your mind and give you a clean, beautiful look. When you add the finishing touches of a label, it takes away the guesswork and gives your mind a break when looking for items. It allows you to simply dance in your space.

It's also key for keeping your organization going. When you put items away, you instantly know where they go, saving you time, frustration, and stress. That's the whole reason we began this organizing journey! It is a part of the process that helps make restoring your space realistically possible.

There are many ways to label, from chalk or window markers to handwrite the category, to a simple label maker, fancy vinyl lettering machine, or pre-printed stickers from The Container Store, Amazon or Etsy. No matter which style works in your budget and aesthetic, you really cannot go wrong. Give yourself grace to play around! Try out a category and style—if you don't like it, try another one! If one category ends up being too specific, try going more broad and vice versa. Remember these are our new dancing shoes, so take time to break them in.

FINAL THOUGHTS

As we close out this part of the process, I know that everyone, especially these days, wants to organize and create systems and be done. Finished. Forever! However, we are living in a world of extreme excess that constantly expands because items are easy to afford and acquire. That's why I chose the word "Cultivate" for this step, because cultivating the right dance for your space is an ongoing process. It's always changing. Our lives and culture are in flux at a rapid pace and that means a system that worked for us yesterday might not work for us today.

You will have new items. They will enter your home. You will need to give them a space in your home and figure out new systems for them. It is also inevitable that life events will happen that throw us off beat in our rhythms. And that's OK! Now you know what to do to get back in step with your dance. Now you have resources and tools—and a mindset—to help you. The key is feeling confident in your skills to organize and remembering Jesus' wise words:

"Don't store up treasures here on earth, where moths eat them and rust destroys them, and where thieves break in and steal. Store your treasures in heaven, where moths and rust cannot destroy, and thieves do not break in and steal. Wherever your treasure is, there the desires of your heart will be also" (Matthew 6:19-21 NLT).

Don't be overwhelmed by this part of the process. Just begin! Make one decision; then make the next decision, and then the next. Before you know it, you'll have choreographed your own beautiful organizing dance! God has given you everything you need to create an organizing system—power to make decisions, love to anchor you, and self-control to cultivate your new systems. 2 Timothy 1:7 reminds us, "For God has not given us a spirit of fear and timidity, but of power, love, and self-discipline" (NLT).

BONUS: CURATE

While you cultivate your organizational dance, you might want to *CURATE* your space with style and design as well! Like genre is to dance, style is to organization. The genre of dance (ballroom, hip-hop, ballet, etc.) adds specific styles, movements, and emotional undertones; it guides the choreography, music, and costumes. Adding a design style you love to your space can help to guide what bins you use, what accent pieces to add, and what colors to focus on to create the feeling you want when you enter the room.

Look back at your notes or journal at the design styles that resonated most with you; then compare them with the items you chose to keep.

My mom gave me a painting of the beach that one of her student's parent's painted in the '70s. It was old and dirty, but I knew I loved it and wanted to keep it. I had it professionally restored. Then, I designed my home office around it, because it had the modern beach aesthetic I was going for. It hangs on the wall and adds style to my space—style that means something personal to me and is a family heirloom.

Examples might include adding a potted plant, or artfully displaying your beloved *Harry Potter* books in your newly decluttered bookcase. It can be that simple! Maybe that set of dishes you chose to keep can now be washed and placed beautifully and strategically in your cupboard! You get the idea. Look at your favorite social media app for styling and design ideas, and add your creative spin to it. These beloved items will finally make sense and become more visible because they are no longer surrounded by the distractions of clutter.

Keep in mind: it's fun to combine new with the old! It honors the past and also who you are now, and gives you momentum and joy for the future. A wonderful, hard-working mom of two came to me because her living room was cluttered and outdated. Anne's goals were to declutter, acquire new couches, and create a desk area with chairs to work and host. She brought me in to help her make decisions about what to keep and what to donate, and to help her learn how to style a space with a more current look.

As I walked through the G.R.A.C.E. method with her, we uncovered heaps of family photos and photo albums. They were buried underneath clutter and mixed in with DVD's and PlayStation games. Can anyone else relate? She looked at her walls, disappointed. The pictures on the walls needed an update, too. She asked, "Melinda, can you help me create a gallery wall?" Excited, I replied "Yes!" I grouped the pictures together in one area until we finished decluttering so that I could a) find them, and b) prepare them for review with Anne at a later time.

Next, she shopped to acquire couches, chairs and a desk, while I sorted her photos and categorized them so we could review and find favorites to use in the living room gallery wall. Anne did great! She knew which photos to get rid of, which to keep, and which ones were favorites she wanted to see every day. We looked at all of her frames and made decisions about those, too, using the "Keep," "Toss," "Donate" categories. We replaced old photos with her newly selected favorite ones for the gallery wall. While going through this process with Anne, I learned that her daughter was an artist and preserved butterflies. These items made Anne extremely proud and happy as a mother. I looked at her daughter's artwork and beautiful butterflies with Anne and helped her pick out her favorites. They are now included in Anne's gallery wall. Together, we curated a beautiful art wall of heirlooms, current photos, artwork, and butterflies.

The new gallery wall, combined with the new furniture and a completely organized room, created a living room that was not only functional but gorgeous. Anne learned how to curate her space and cultivate new organizing habits. That's life-changing stuff!

Many times, curating a space is much simpler, and no new products need to be bought at all! Krystal reached out to me to help her with her closet. She has a toddler and owns and runs her own business. She wanted to be able to get dressed quickly, know where things are, and to put outfits away neatly in her walk-in closet. Her life is, in general, stressful, so I knew I wanted her closet to bring a smile to her face and be a place of ease.

I got her closet in tip-top organizational shape and still had room on some shelves. I decided to curate the shelves with a few family photos, trendy hats, cool glass jars, and jewelry trays. All of these items she had chosen to keep either because she loved them, or they had a special meaning to her. I simply placed them in a beautiful way and kept the integrity of how she used those shelves every day. I curated what she already had—no new bins required.

PLAY

I'm also a big believer in play and creativity. Even as adults, we need to be reminded that it's OK to play. Julia Cameron explains, "If you play, you will get ideas. When people play, they're actually spoiling themselves a little bit. They're being kind and tender toward themselves." [33] She tells us to, "Do what intrigues you, explore what interests you; think mystery, not mastery." [34]

That's what curating a space is to me. It's my time to play and add a sense of childlike whimsy and fun to a room. When I decorated my home office, I included several items from my childhood that spark a sense of play and creativity in me as a reminder to actually stop and play! My bookshelves have bells from places I've been and theatre masks that mark the special moments in my life when I was acting on the stage. My desk has a little gold stamp to make wax seals. I've never used it as an actual wax stamp, but I used it all the time growing up in my dollhouses as décor. These little nods to my imaginative childhood-self gives my office a sense of whimsy and play.

I incorporate this idea with my clients whenever I can, too! Remember that gallery wall I curated for Anne? That's why I also styled the wall with her daughter's artwork and beautiful butterflies—it adds creativity, imagination and play. This childlike energy my clients have slowly lost over time due to clutter and chaos, I help recover. I challenge you to do the same when you *CULTIVATE* and curate your space. Add whimsy! Add play! Add fun! Add a sense of you and your inner child.

PRAYER

Thank you, Lord, for the items you've helped me decide to keep. They are a blessing from you because they help me live out your purpose for my life. Thank you that I have space to store and organize these items. Be with me as I give them each a home. Show me how to place them in such a way that is efficient and supports my family's natural rhythms. Give me discipline to create my organizing dance and to maintain it. I confess that I will need your help to continue to stand firm and to not submit to the power of "stuff and clutter." I call on your love to anchor me and hold me as I *CULTIVATE* organization and ease during these ever-changing times.

REFLECT

Journal. Take a few minutes to ponder and write in your journal. Consider the space you are currently organizing. What systems do you need to put in place to help your dance in the space become more efficient? What challenges are standing in your way of cultivating a new organizing dance?

DEEP DIVE

Dance.

- Put all your items away.

- Create an organizing system that works for you!

- Take an after photo and tag me on Instagram: @melindagraceorganizing, #organizingdance.

BONUS: Curate your space! Revisit your dream space. What design styles do you love? Add style and finishing touches. Example: Hang a picture that ties the space together. Add a basket or plant.

HOME OFFICE

The home office is often a cross between personal life and work life. It can contain papers, photos, legal documents, and business plans all in one place. It is the room where I think cultivating your own dance and rhythms is essential—because it's the room that holds you and your family's life! Here's my list of Top 10 Tips to help you cultivate your organizing dance in your home office. You can download more "Home Office" resources at melindagrace.com/grace.

1. Create zones for each category used in your office

2. Determine which category is used or accessed daily, monthly, quarterly, yearly

3. Place categories used daily within reach on the most accessible drawer or shelf

4. Place categories used less often up high or in the back

5. Keep personal categories in separate zones from business categories

6. Actually go through your paper clutter

7. Minimize paperwork by scanning files and requesting electronic bills and statements

WEEK SIX

ENJOY

"... there is nothing better than to be happy and enjoy ourselves as long as we can. And people should eat and drink and enjoy the fruits of their labor, for these are gifts from God."

Ecclesiastes 3:12-13 (NLT)

Finally, we come to the end of our G.R.A.C.E. journey, and it's time to **ENJOY** the fruits of our labors!

Our backyard is a tall hill that opens up to the Santa Monica Mountains. The hill is covered in rosemary and is home to gophers, birds, bees, and who knows what else! One night my husband and I were both feeling extremely grateful; so, we hiked up our steep hill to the top, chairs and wine in hand. We sat at the top of the hill overlooking the neighborhood in front of us—the freeway to the left of us, the gorgeous Santa Monica Mountains and California oak trees behind us. A 360-degree view of gorgeousness! I was enjoying this moment in every part of my body, mind and soul! After a year of being in our new house, doing all the designing, coordinating, renovating, unpacking, and organizing, my husband and I gave ourselves a reward by taking a moment to ENJOY the fruits of our labors and the gifts God had given us!

FACT

"Studies show that people who got a little treat, in the form of receiving a surprise gift or watching a funny video, gained in self-control. It's a Secret of Adulthood: If I give more to myself, I can ask more from myself. Self-regard isn't selfish."

Gretchen Rubin, Psych Central[35]

CELEBRATE

Sometimes you may feel guilty or frivolous for stopping to be thankful and enjoying life, God's blessings, and the rewards of our hard work; but, did you know that it's a Biblical principle?

". . . there is nothing better than to be happy and enjoy ourselves as long as we can. And people should eat and drink and enjoy the fruits of their labor, for these are gifts from God" (Ecclesiastes 3:12-13 NLT). In our fast-paced world, it may be hard to pause for a moment, reflect and feel all the feels; but, in this final step of the G.R.A.C.E. process, you're going to do just that by thanking God and enjoying the work we've done through His provision, grace, and power.

I'm reminded of the classic Bible story of God resting on the seventh day. "Then God looked over all he had made, and he saw that it was very good!" (Gen 1:31 NLT). He took a moment, a second, a millisecond (however time works in God's realm) to see that the work He created was not just good, but VERY good. I'm sure He also celebrated in a God-sized way all of His handiwork! So, take time to celebrate and ENJOY the amazing work you have done over the last six weeks! Sit in the space and relish how it makes you feel.

In this final step, you are also going to revisit your goals, reflect on how far you've come, and **give yourself a reward that you *ENJOY*** for completing your goals and shifting the energy and focus in your home. This may be a step you don't want to do simply because it seems too easy, and you might be thinking, *What's the point? I'm finished. My space is organized. Bye!* But, wait! Remember those feelings you wanted to feel when your space was organized and styled? This is it. This is that moment!

Celebrate your success with a reward of your choosing. It can be big or small, free or costly. Anyone watch the TV show *Parks and*

Recreation? Remember the episode, "Pawnee Rangers," where Retta & Tom create a new tradition called "Treat Yo Self" day? Apparently, this pop culture spin is legit. "When we give ourselves treats, we feel energized, cared for, and contented, which boosts our self-command—and self-command helps us maintain our healthy habits." [36] In the words of the characters Retta & Tom, "Treat Yo Self." Call your best friend, buy some flowers to put in your newly organized space, make a cup of tea (my favorite!), or go for a walk. Whatever makes you smile and feel celebratory—DO THAT! Enjoy accomplishing your organizational goals! This will inspire you to keep cultivating your rhythms in the space and hopefully give you the confidence to tackle the next organizing project in your home or office.

Having a beautiful, organized space will bring you joy that you often can't keep quiet about. Lainey hired me to unpack her newly renovated house. I'll always remember the day that I focused solely on the kitchen and pantry. Lainey popped in and out of unpacking while she also worked to get things squared away with the contractor and architect. It was a long eight-hour day and at the end of it, she was so excited about how the kitchen and pantry were coming together that she called her daughter and had her bring over her adorable grandson! She was celebrating with those closest to her, and it was fun for me to watch her show off her newly organized kitchen and pantry. I was so proud and honored to celebrate with her.

It can be that simple of a celebration! Lainey's reward was seeing her grandson in her home, walking around and playing. Celebration is powerful. Charles Spurgeon said, "It is not how much we have, but how much we enjoy, that makes happiness." Enjoy your newly organized space. "Sing and make music from your heart to the Lord, always giving thanks to God the Father for everything, in the name of the Lord Jesus Christ" (Ephesians 5:19-20 NIV). He said to give thanks for "everything." That includes your beautifully organized space, all the curated items in it, the cultivated dances, hard work, strength, wisdom and creativity God gave you—everything.

And now I say, THANK YOU! Thank you for going on your organizing journey with me. It's been so much fun to cheer you on and be your guide. Please stay in touch and reach out with your organizing successes and questions.

PRAYER

Thank you, Lord, that the plans of the diligent lead to profit. You have helped me to be diligent and conquer my clutter and style my space(s). You have guided me as I literally threw off the physical items that were hindering me from moving forward in my life goals and my relationship with you. Thank you for setting me free from the bondage of needless, worthless physical clutter. I praise you for the gift of space and for the chosen items in this space. I see that it is very good! I praise you for my new clarity of purpose, renewed relationships, increase in energy, and the calm that I feel in this moment. Lord, Jesus, I am grateful for your mercies that are new every morning and that lead me to a newfound freedom and focus. Amen.

REFLECT

Journal. Take a few minutes to write in your journal about this organizing experience over the past six weeks. What are two words that describe your "before" state and your "after" mindset?

Share. If you're feeling brave on social media, post a pic on Instagram, tag me, and use #mgograce so I can celebrate with you!

DEEP DIVE

Celebrate.

- STOP! Take a moment to *ENJOY* your newly organized space.

- Give yourself a special reward for completing your organizing goals!

7 WAYS TO ENJOY

Stopping to smell the roses and enjoy life's little gifts can be hard in our modern world. Here are some ideas to inspire you to slow down and take it all in.

1. Acquire fresh flowers and put them in a beautiful vase
2. Make a delicious cup of tea (my favorite!)
3. Grab a book and read it
4. Journal about gratitude
5. Invite a friend over
6. Play a board game with your kids
7. Cook your favorite meal and serve it on your most beautiful dishes

AFTERWORD: RESTORE

"He restores my soul;
He leads me in the paths of righteousness
For His name's sake"

Psalm 23:3 (NKJV)

Many of you will find it tough to actually start the organizing process. Starting can be THE hardest thing. It's like going to the gym. It's so hard to just get there, but when you do, it feels *soooo* good. If you have found it hard to simply get started, please reach out to me! I offer virtual and in-person organizing services to relieve your stress and create a sanctuary you love.

You can find me online: melindagrace.com or on Instagram: instagram.com/melindagraceorganizing.

For others, the hardest part is going to be "maintaining" your newly organized space. Now that we've gotten to know each other over six weeks, may I be honest here? I hate the word "maintain." It's boring, two-dimensional, business-y and, frankly, it's organizer speak. Many of you don't have the time or energy to run around your house putting everything away, in every room, every day. So, let's break this up.

I propose a different take on this concept. For me, organizing is and has always been an activity that grounds me. It *RESTORES* me. It puts me in the present and allows me to work with my hands, get off the computer and take a break from social media. Like those of you who take a yoga class, or read the Bible or go for a run because it grounds you and revives your soul, may I offer to you that organizing can do the same?

Don't think of it as something you have to do, something your expert organizer is requesting you do, or a chore reminiscent of the days when your mom ordered you to dust the mantle or vacuum the living room so that you'd grow up to be a productive adult. Rather, think of it as a restorative dance of self-care.

Anxiety in some form or fashion is something I've worked with my whole life because I'm a highly sensitive, adventurous planner, and a 7 on the enneagram chart! I like to set goals, plan, and schedule— then throw all of that out the window to go on a fun adventure. I'm constantly thinking about the future, and I bet most of you are, too. Anxiety builds up when we are too focused on the future and fearful of outcomes that haven't happened yet. I know from personal experience that taking the time to put my items away and keep up my organization puts me in the present and offers a release from the pressures of this world.

Personally, I stop to *RESTORE* my space when I feel the anxiety building up, when my spirit gets restless—when my heart is looking for direction and can't find it. I do this as a restorative act of self-care. I often find that after I've put my space in order again, I can breathe easier and rest. So, that's what I propose. I propose you switch your mindset from, "I have to maintain this space in a given timeframe" to "I want to restore this space as my dance of self-care at the time that I need it."

And then you do that! You do one thing that will rejuvenate your space. I like to *RESTORE* my space fifteen minutes at a time. I tell myself, *Do this one thing for fifteen minutes.* It's not that long. And then I wind up having so much fun that my fifteen minutes have turned into hours.

Restoration at this point should be easy because everything has a home. It's simply putting items back where they belong. Even if you're limited on time, taking five minutes here and five minutes there every day to put a few things back in their homes is a game changer. Here are some ideas of quick wins to restore a room that you have organized:

 The easiest clutter to build up is mail. Take five minutes each day to go through your mail and disperse each piece to its next home and action step. Most mail can go in the trash, as a lot of information can be found online. For our home, I like to keep this month's paper bill in a file, and the previous month's, I shred. You may want to go paperless and therefore it's no longer a physical source of clutter. You definitely need a spot where mail goes that you can deal with at a later date. For me, it's on my home office desk in a cute in-box. This way when you go through the mail, it's fast. Trash, File, or In-box. Done.

 Another area where clutter accumulates fast is the bedroom. I have yet to meet a person that loves putting clothes away, folded or hung. In complete honesty, I don't put my clothes away every day. I put them away about every week. Have a spot where you can put them or hang them that's out of the way. Then, when you have a pocket of time that week, actually put them away. Set a timer for 15 minutes if that helps you. Make it a game with your kids—with a reward. Who can put their clothes away the fastest? Ready, set, go!

 The kitchen in my home seems to be the area that gets the messiest the fastest. I do wash the dishes once a day or every other day. That's now the longest part of the process. Putting them away is a breeze because every single kitchen item has a home. If it doesn't belong in the kitchen, it goes to the room where it does belong. I give myself lots of grace in the kitchen. One, because I'm not the best cook! Two, because I'm

always creating a new dance in my kitchen based on our current diet and efficiency. I'd say about once a year, I rethink my layout, declutter, and hunt for ten items I can release. It's not stressful. It's an act of restoration that helps me inside and out.

 Many of my clients are working moms, so a playroom or a kid's room is recipe for disaster . . . real quick. Kids will be kids. Give them an area where they can get messy, creative, and imaginative. Since you've organized their room or playroom with my G.R.A.C.E. method, every toy has a home and every bin has a label. I like general category bins and labels with colorful pictures of that category, so even a little one can put their toys away quickly. I remember as a kid, putting my toys and stuffed animals away before a guest came over, before holidays, or before school started again in the fall. It's up to you how often to take 15–30 minutes to put the toys away based on your threshold for clutter. My only advice is to use this act of restoration to teach your children about organization while also making it fun! You can download more "Playroom" resources at melindagrace.com/grace.

 The other room of the house I restore more frequently is my home office, and I recommend you do, too, if this room houses bills, computers, calendars, work and school papers. Process bills as they come in either as an email or mail. Or add it to your calendar before the due date. I spend five to ten minutes a day tidying my home office. Again, it's easy because I have set up clearly labeled files, zoned drawers and shelves, and have bins for everything I need in my office. The most common thing I restore is my desk because I have a ton of ideas for my organizing company that I write on anything and everything I can find. If maintaining your home office and papers takes more than 15–30 minutes at a time, then either you're waiting too long to restore this space or you need to go through the G.R.A.C.E. process again and fine-tune.

At the end of an organizing project, I give my clients simple tips and tricks to restore a space that is custom to them and how they function. A lot of clients get it, and they're off to the races. Others, it's just not their jam. Period. End of story. There is a silver lining! Did you know that you can hire someone else to do the restoration part of organizing for you? Yep. Like your consistent cleaning person, many organizers like myself offer a "maintenance organizing" package. Hire me to come restore your previously organized space a couple times a month or a couple times a year, depending on your schedule and budget. It's amazing! Go to melindagrace.com/restore to learn more.

Or maybe you want your own detailed map with tasks to do every day, week, month, quarterly, and yearly. Simply go to melindagrace. com/grace for restoration organizing ideas. Try it out. It may work for you and be the best thing since sliced bread! I have a few daily and weekly restoring tasks that I do, and they work great for me and our home.

However, if you get frustrated that you can't keep up or forgot this month's task because life got crazy and hiring an organizer is out of the question, BREATHE. Forget the list. Do you. Do your dance. You got this. Give yourself pockets of five to 15 minutes, and let restoring your home be a gentler, kinder approach. Give yourself grace! Life gets hectic and throws us curveballs. Clutter also comes in waves: a busy work season, the holidays, new school routines, a health diagnosis. Honestly, I do find that in those times, I cherish my five to 15 minutes that are all mine. Sometimes I use them to journal, pray, read, watch an inspiring video, and other times I use that five minutes to "feed the cat."

"Feed the cat?" you ask? Yep. In my acting days, I worked at a Christian Theater Company in Houston. The founder and artistic director would offer devotionals to resident staff and actors. I'll never forget one of the stories she told about a time she was going through when she was not sure of what to do next and was waiting on God for direction. The only thing she knew to do and heard God say was: "Feed the cat." And she did. She went home and fed her cat. Or at least that's how I remember the story, and that's how it landed in my spirit that morning of the devotional.

I've carried her example with me for over 20 years, and when things get crazy or I'm waiting on God and getting restless, I hear that artist's words, "Feed the cat." And I do. I will literally feed my cat. This is also a metaphor for doing the small, mundane tasks that must be done sometimes. If you don't feed the cat, guess what will happen? It's in those small, everyday tasks that big change can happen—where emotional and spiritual restoration can happen. So again, I encourage you, let this part of the process RESTORE you.

Let it be an act of healing!

FINAL PRAYER

Dear God,

Thank you for walking with me as I reclaim my home, time, and relationship with you. Be with me as I work to keep the chaos, overwhelm, and stress at an arm's length so I can move about each day, full of your new mercies, with grace and love. "Restore to me the joy of your salvation, and grant me a willing spirit, to sustain me" (Psalm 51:12 NIV). Let healing and restoration be the new song of my home. Let joy overflow and love abound.

Amen.

FINAL REFLECTION

Whether this is your first time completing the G.R.A.C.E. method or your fiftieth, my prayer for you is that of David's in Psalm 51:12: "Restore to me the joy of your salvation, and grant me a willing spirit, to sustain me" (NIV). May God restore and sustain you, always. Thank YOU for allowing me to be a part of your organizing journey—one that hopefully helped bring you closer to your calling and purpose in God, by clearing out the noise and literally throwing "off everything that hinders" (Hebrews 12:1 NIV).

REFERENCES

1. Austin, Daryl (2024 January 11). "Being organized can actually improve mental health. This is why." Retrieved from **https://www.nationalgeographic.com/premium/article/organizing-clutter-mental-health#:**

2. Chatzky, Jean (2017 May 31). "One in Four Americans Has a Clutter Problem - And Could Be Sitting on Some Serious Cash." Retrieved from **https://www.nbcnews.com/business/personal-finance/one-four-americans-has-clutter-problem-could-be-sitting-some-n766681**

3. Wallman, James (2015 Jan 24). "Viewpoint: The Hazards of Too Much Stuff." Retrieved from **https://www.bbc.com/news/magazine-30849473**

4. Rush, Ryan (2022 Jan 2). "Fruit of the Spirit: Self Control." Retrieved from **https://vimeo.com/661780493**

5. Pforzheimer, Adrian & Alexander Truelove (2021 Sept 29) "Trash in America: Moving from Destructive Consumption Towards a Zero-Waste System." Retrieved from **https://frontiergroup.org/reports/fg/trash-america-0**

6. Pforzheimer, Adrian & Alexander Truelove (2021 Sept 29) "Trash in America: Moving from Destructive Consumption Towards a Zero-Waste System." Retrieved from **https://frontiergroup.org/reports/fg/trash-america-0**

7. University of Exeter (2018 May 15). "Evidence Shows Ocean Sound May Help Reduce Stress and Create a Sense of Calm." Retrieved from **https://phys.org/news/2018-05-evidence-ocean-stress-calm.html**

8. Zuidgeest, Tim (2021 July 21). "Neuromarketing; Here's Everything You Need To Know". Retrieved from **https://www.newneuromarketing.com/neuromarketing**

9. Le Beau Lucchesi, Emilie (2019 Jan 3). "The Unbearable Heaviness of Clutter." The New York Times. Retrieved from **https://www.nytimes.com/2019/01/03/well/mind/clutter-stress-procrastination-psychology.html**

10. Fuller, Kristen MD (2022 June 30). "The Negative Impact of Clutter on Mental Health." Retrieved from **https://www.verywellmind.com/decluttering-our-house-to-cleanse-our-minds-5101511**

11. Wallman, James (2015 Jan 24). "Viewpoint: The Hazards of Too Much Stuff." Retrieved from **https://www.bbc.com/news/magazine-30849473**

12. Pixie Technology (2017 May 02). "Lost and Found: The Average American Spends 2.5 Days Each Year Looking For Lost Items Collectively Costing U.S. Households $2.7 Billion Annually in Replacement Costs." Retrieved from **https://www.prnewswire.com/news-releases/lost-and-found-the-average-american-spends-25-days-each-year-looking-for-lost-items-collectively-costing-us-households-27-billion-annually-in-replacement-costs-300449305.html**

13. Tulane University. "Understanding the Effects of Social Isolation on Mental Health." (2020 Dec 8). Retrieved from **https://publichealth.tulane.edu/blog/effects-of-social-isolation-on-mental-health/**

14. Freeman, Emily P. "Becoming A Soul Minimalist." Retrieved from **https://emilypfreeman.com/becoming-soul-minimalist/**

15. Lotito, Jennifer. (2024 Jan 10). "How To Set SMART 2024 Goals." Retrieved from **https://www.forbes.com/sites/jenniferlotito/2024/01/10/how-to-set-smart-2024-goals/?sh=10b9459fe2a9**

16. Ziglar, Zig (1982). See You at the Top. Pelican Publishing.

17. Doran, George T. (1981 November). "There's a S.M.A.R.T. way to write management's goals and objectives." Retrieved from **https://community.mis.temple.edu/mis0855002fall2015/files/2015/10/S.M.A.R.T-Way-Management-Review.pdf**

18. Robbins, Tony. Retrieved from **https://www.tonyrobbins.com/tony-robbins-quotes/**

19. Wikipedia: **https://en.wikipedia.org/wiki/Circular_economy**

20. Buy Nothing Project **https://buynothingproject.org**

21. Sills, Judith Ph.D. (2014 November 4). "Let It Go!". Retrieved from **https://www.psychologytoday.com/us/articles/201411/let-it-go**

22. Swindoll, Charles. (2019 May 27). "An Appraisal." Retrieved from **https://insight.org/resources/daily-devotional/individual/an-appraisal1**

23. Cameron, J., & Bryan, M. A. (1992). The Artist's Way: A Spiritual Path to Higher Creativity. New York, NY, G.P. Putnam's Sons.

24. Wikipedia: **https://en.wikipedia.org/wiki/Kinesthetic_sympathy**

25. Chaplain Kevin Deegan. Mental Wellness Course. 2020. **https://www.bewellresourcesla.com**

26. Terkeurst, Lysa. (2014 February 21). "The Secret For Unleashing God's Peace in Your Situation - #Beanoticer." Retrieved from **https://lysaterkeurst.com/2014/02/21/the-secret-for-unleashing-gods-peace-in-your-situation-beanoticer/**

27. Merriam-Webster Dictionary: **https://www.merriam-webster.com/dictionary/contented**

28. Bonhoeffer, Dietrich. (2010). Letters and Papers from Prison. Minneapolis, MN, Fortress Press.

29. Tozer, A.W. Signposts: A Collection of Sayings from A.W. Tozer. Compiled by Harry Verploegh. Wheaton, IL: Victor Books, 1988.

30. UCLA Health. (2023 March 22). "Health benefits of gratitude." Retrieved from **https://www.uclahealth.org/news/article/health-benefits-gratitude**

31. Press Release. (2016 June 14). "The Container Store Enhances Customer Experience and Operational Productivity with Nationwide Rollout of Theatro's Voice-Controlled Wearable." The Container Store. Retrieved from

2

https://investor.containerstore.com/press-releases/press-release-details/2016/The-Container-Store-Enhances-Customer-Experience-and-Operational-Productivity-with-Nationwide-Rollout-of-Theatros-Voice-Controlled-Wearable/default.aspx

32. Dance is human behaviour composed (from the dancer's perspective, which is usually shared by the audience members of the dancer's culture) of purposeful (individual choice and social learning play a role), intentionally rhythmical, and culturally patterned sequences of nonverbal body movement mostly other than those performed in ordinary motor activities. The motion (in time, space, and with effort) has an inherent and aesthetic value (the notion of appropriateness and competency as viewed by the dancer's culture) and symbolic potential.[2]   Judith Lynne Hanna (1983). *The performer-audience connection: emotion to metaphor in dance and society.* University of Texas Press. ISBN 978-0-292-76478-1

33. Wilding, Melody. (2021 January 4). "How To Make Listening Your Superpower, According to Bestselling Author Julia Cameron." Retrieved from **https://www.forbes.com/sites/melodywilding/2021/01/04/how-to-make-listening-your-superpower-according-to-bestselling-author-julia-cameron/**

34. Cameron, J., & Bryan, M. A. (1992). The Artist's Way: A Spiritual Path to Higher Creativity. New York, NY, G.P. Putnam's Sons.

35. Rubin, Gretchen. (2014 December 13). "The Psychology of Rewarding Yourself with Treats." Retrieved from **https://psychcentral.com/blog/psychology-rewarding-yourself-with-treats#1**

36. Rubin, Gretchen. (2014 December 13). "The Psychology of Rewarding Yourself with Treats." Retrieved from **https://psychcentral.com/blog/psychology-rewarding-yourself-with-treats#1**

INSPIRATION

Need to renew your inspiration to get started or keep you going? Have fun "window shopping" at these websites, Instagram pages, and stores. Adding a new, beautiful basket or picture as you organize or restore a space can bring a smile to your face and light up a room!

WORTHY WEBSITES

MAGNOLIA
magnolia.com

STUDIO MCGEE
studio-mcgee.com

DAYSPRING
dayspring.com

INSPIRING INSTAGRAMS

@escape.to.the.chateau & @thestrawbridgefamily
@mariekondo
@magnolia
@studiomcgee
@beautifulmesshome
@smartinthekitchen

@perigold
@feastvintage
@emilypfreeman
@dayspringcards
@apricotlanefarms
@hertrueworth
@cultivatewhatmatters
@laur_akins
@gmoulin_limitededitions
@laracasey

STYLISH SHOPS

THE CONTAINER STORE
containerstore.com

CRATE & BARREL
crateandbarrel.com

PERIGOLD
perigold.com

SERENA & LILY
serenaandlily.com

MCGEE & CO.
mcgeeandco.com

A BEAUTIFUL MESS HOME & GARDEN
abeautifulmesshome.com

BEAUTIFUL BRANDS

CULTIVATE WHAT MATTERS
cultivatewhatmatters.com

BIGSO
bigso.com

PROKEEPER by Progressive
progressiveintl.com

IDESIGN
idesignlivesimply.com

MARIAGEFRERE
mariagefreres.com

ABOUT THE AUTHOR

Melinda Grace is a professional organizer and lifelong follower of Christ. Realizing that grace, home, and faith were everything to her, she started an organizing business to help others declutter and reconnect with their calling. She works with clients in Los Angeles and Ventura County, turning their homes into sanctuaries to find peace and rediscover faith. She is passionate about the intersection of faith and organizing and hopes this book brings clarity and connection with your faith. Melinda loves to go the beach with her husband and hug her cat, Tango.

You can find out more about Melinda at <u>melindagrace.com</u>.

Are you looking for an organizing expert to feature on your podcast, event, or show?

Connect with Melinda Grace now to book a fun, heartfelt speaker! Her signature organizing talks center around her G.R.A.C.E. organizing method, as well as her and her clients' own experiences with organizing, and will leave guests inspired, ready and armed with the knowledge they need to tackle their clutter.

If you enjoyed this book, please consider leaving a positive review on Amazon and Goodreads and getting a copy for a friend.